THE PEAKY BLINDERS QUIZ BOOK

THE PEAKY BLINDERS QUIZ BOOK

JOE SHOOMAN

bl!nk

First published in the UK in 2025 by Blink Publishing
An imprint of Bonnier Books UK
5th Floor, HYLO, 105 Bunhill Row,
London, EC1Y 8LZ

A CIP catalogue record for this book is available from the British Library.

Hardback ISBN: 9781785128684

1 3 5 7 9 10 8 6 4 2

Design and Typeset by Envy Design Ltd
Printed and bound in Great Britain by Clays Ltd, Elcograf S.p.A.

The authorised representative in the EEA is
Bonnier Books UK (Ireland) Limited.
Registered office address: Floor 3, Block 3, Miesian Plaza,
Dublin 2, D02 Y754, Ireland
compliance@bonnierbooks.ie

www.bonnierbooks.co.uk

CONTENTS

SERIES FOUR

SERIES FIVE

SERIES SIX

INTRODUCTION

Let us ask you a couple of questions:

How far would you go to make sure your family was set for life?
How far would you go to make sure nobody messed with them?

We reckon we know the answer to both:

To the ends of the earth, right?

If needed, you'd bend or break laws and rules to keep your tribe from being cheated, defeated, treated like rubbish and trodden down. We all would. So given that we're in agreement that morality is inherently flexible dependent on context, we must look at Thomas Shelby as an exemplar of family loyalty and love. After all, ultimately everything he does is for the greater good of the

Shelby family and its businesses, be his actions legitimate or otherwise in the feebly unmoving eyes of the law.

It gets more complicated however because there are more questions we must ask:

Would you kill for your family?

Would you kill for the businesses?

The top one's almost certainly a yes but the second... well, hmm, that's where lines start to blur and things get a little more tricky. That's where the Shelby family becomes the Peaky Blinders. That's where people start to disappear and eyes start getting taken in order to send messages to other people who are trying to harm your people. That's where an almost-insurmountable tension lies, and that's where this most human of shows gets a fair amount of its narrative drive. Because in actual real life nothing is black and white, not entirely, and in those interim shades of grey there are numerous justifications, unruly problems and – let's be honest – huge profits to be made.

In the aftermath of a brutal and brutalising Great War, a generation of young men returned home profoundly changed, their ethical compasses skewed forever by the sheer horror of what they had been told to do.

Thomas et al. are products of their experiences – and that brings both great knowledge and terrifying aspects into their lives. Ex-soldiers, now thrown back into a world that's also changed and changing ever-faster, each one still carrying the unutterable weight of memories of carnage, of the dehumanising madness that they have been through. How could anyone hope to adjust? And what of those left behind to keep things ticking over?

Peaky Blinders takes that theme and expands it. When Tommy joined the war, he was a happy lad who wanted nothing more than to work with horses and to fall in love. After the war, he's a hard-headed, quietly spoken, terrifying chief schemer, enforcer and voracious money-chaser. He, like so many others, has realised that the line between the good guys and the baddies is anything but solid. In fact, sometimes being a good guy means playing with some dark, dangerous forces. Perhaps the winners and the good guys aren't the same after all. Another lesson from the trenches: know your enemy. Perhaps he's not the man covered in mud and blood across no man's land. Perhaps he's the one in a pristine general's uniform, stationed several miles away in a safe, warm command position. Perhaps it's those who created the conditions in which so many lives were twisted and broken and thrown away at the whim of a warmonger. Perhaps, perhaps, perhaps... So many questions. Maybe the answers that are found through war are not useful, as they are more damaging than the sweetness of ignorance.

Peaky Blinders is rightly held to be one of the greatest British series of all time. Here, we've delved into the magic and madness of this tremendous drama to put together a quiz book that covers not only the TV episodes but also the careers of many of the key actors involved.

Life is about light and shade, of course, so there's a plethora of games and challenges included here too. You don't have to be a Blinders geek to play these ones – in fact, you don't need to know much about the show at all. There's something here, we reckon, for everyone. So lest we get bogged down in the mud of gnarliness, let's remember a couple of things:

One way to keep family and friends close is to laugh together.
A great way to laugh together is to play together.

We offer this book in that unquenchable spirit of togetherness, and promise that no gorgeous, helpful, majestic horses were harmed in the making of it. We could learn a lot from those glorious beasts. Let's saddle up and get trotting...

In the bleak mid-winter
Frosty wind made moan
Earth stood hard as iron,
Water like a stone;
Snow had fallen, snow on snow,
Snow on snow,
In the bleak mid-winter
Long ago.

– *Christina Rossetti, 1872*

SERIES ONE

SERIES ONE:
EPISODE ONE

It begins: we meet the Shelby family, post-World War I, a major family of bookmakers who are feared on the streets of Small Heath in Birmingham. Arthur is de facto leader of the family but it's very clear that actually his brother Tommy is way sharper and more ambitious. But the Shelbys and their gang, the Peaky Blinders, are also attracting the wrong kind of attention...

1. A Chinese fortune teller blows some powder into the face of the horse. What colour?
   a. Red
   b. Blue
   c. Yellow

2. For what reason?
   a. To cure the horse of illness
   b. To make it win the race
   c. As a warning against witches

3. What's the name of the horse?
   a. Monkey Boy
   b. Kempton Lass
   c. Monaghan Boy

4. Tommy surprises his brother Finn when he gets home. But how old is the young lad?
   a. Ten
   b. Eleven
   c. Eight

5. When Arthur questions Tommy about the latter's motives, what does Tommy say in reply?
   a. 'None of your business, old man'
   b. 'I think, Arthur… so you don't have to'
   c. 'I know what I'm doing… unlike some'

6. And what's Arthur's parting shot?
   a. That there's trouble coming
   b. That betting is a mug's game
   c. That times are going to get easy

7. What does Freddie drink in the pub?
   a. Bitter
   b. Lager
   c. Mild

8. And what does Freddie ask Tommy?
   a. Why they always drink in the same pub
   b. Why their names are on 'a list' together
   c. Why Tommy never joined the Communists

9. But there's something historical that binds the men together strongly, nonetheless. What is it?
   a. Tommy bought Freddie's family a house after the war
   b. Freddie tipped Tommy off that Monaghan Boy was a good horse
   c. Freddie saved Tommy from taking a bullet in France

10. How do we meet Danny Whizz-Bang for the first time?
   a. He rushes into the pub believing he's a bomb that needs to go bang
   b. He dashes across the pub and jumps through a closed window
   c. He throws a hand grenade at a policeman and runs away

11. Freddie and Tommy together restrain Danny. What advice does Tommy have for Danny?
   a. To go home to his wife and clear the smoke and mud from his head
   b. To go home to his wife and kids and prepare to get out of Birmingham
   c. To get away from the pub immediately and never come back

12. What does Tommy announce as he leaves the pub?
   a. That Danny is now barred until further notice
   b. That the Peaky Blinders will take care of the bill
   c. That someone's going to pay for all this mess

13. What does it say on the flyer that Arthur produces?
   a. That these are dangerous times and the church is the answer
   b. That nobody must go out after 10 o'clock from now on
   c. If people are over five foot tall and can fight, they should come to Birmingham

14. Why?
   a. Because the world has turned away from God
   b. Because there are rumours that there will be an air strike
   c. Because the police are recruiting special officers to join them

15. How does Tommy already know about all this?
    a. He's asked the policemen who are already on the Blinders' payroll
    b. He's already spoken with the new chief inspector
    c. He has heard many rumours about it in the pub

16. Aunt Polly speaks with Tommy in the church. What does Tommy tell her?
    a. That his men were supposed to steal four petrol motorcycles but got drunk and picked up the wrong crate
    b. That he's going to bash the heads of the new Specials together because they've got a huge cheek coming here and throwing their weight about
    c. That he's the only man who can make sense of all this nonsense and that people should trust him

17. What did they find when they opened the crate?
    a. Liquor
    b. Guns
    c. Cigarettes

18. From which part of Ireland is Grace?
    a. Galway
    b. Cork
    c. Dublin

19. Arthur is arrested. Where?
   a. At the dog track
   b. In the cinema
   c. At home

20. What's Inspector Campbell's idea for the Peaky Blinders?
   a. That they disband and become part of his crew
   b. That they eliminate the Chinese gangs immediately
   c. That they act as spies for the police

21. What's Campbell's response when Churchill says he likes his hat?
   a. He says thank you and that it's made out of beaver
   b. He says thank you and that it was a two-for-one offer
   c. He frowns because he thinks Churchill is joking

22. Where does Tommy tell an aghast Charlie to take the guns?
   a. To a lock-up mooring on Gas Street
   b. To a lock-up mooring in Manchester
   c. To a lock-up mooring in Tobacco Wharf

23. Campbell enters the museum. Who, unexpectedly, does he talk to as an undercover colleague?
   a. Grace
   b. John
   c. Charlie

24. What rank do we find out, through Danny, that Tommy was?
   a. Colonel
   b. Rear gunner
   c. Sergeant major

25. Why is Tommy relaxed that Monaghan Boy won the race?
   a. It is part of a much longer-term strategy to bring in a thousand pounds' worth of bets, at which point that final race will be fixed so it doesn't win
   b. Tommy had made sure that all of the people put all their money on the horse, so the Blinders had enough liquid assets to invest in copper
   c. He owned the horse, so the stud fees are going to go through the roof from that day forward

SERIES ONE:
EPISODE TWO

Horses, cars, police raids and potential gang wars… things are certainly hotting up in the Blinders' world. There's also love in the air, after a fashion, and a forbidden romance is brought to light. Yup, Episode Two doesn't pull any punches…

1. What consolation prize does Tommy offer in his game with Johnny Dogs?
    a. A spin in the car
    b. A race tip
    c. Safe passage

2. Which three Shelby boys are present? (No multiple choice this time!)

3. What insult provokes the Shelby lads into a fight with the Lees?
   a. 'His mother was a Didicoy whore'
   b. 'He's a true Brit to his core'
   c. 'Birmingham is a place of filth'

4. Freddie and Ada are together, but who demands entry to the house?
   a. Polly Shelby
   b. Campbell's Specials
   c. The Lee boys

5. What time and place does Campbell say he wants to talk to the boss?
   a. In the pub, Friday night at 8pm
   b. At the races, first light
   c. Lickey Tea Rooms, Friday at 10 o'clock

6. Why doesn't Tommy go with the rest, to hand out cash to the wrecked pubs?
   a. He's keeping a low profile to avoid arrest
   b. He's not interested in a few poxy boozers
   c. He's going to stable the horse at Charlie's

7. Rather than talk to Campbell, what does Tommy say will happen?
   a. They will strike back first
   b. He would rather talk to the horse
   c. He'd rather go back to France

8. But what does said striking back involve?
   a. Sending Campbell a single finger in the post
   b. Arranging a bonfire to burn pictures of the King
   c. Arranging a different meeting place

9. Who has Tommy arranged to meet at the fire?
   a. A corrupt policeman
   b. A newspaper reporter
   c. Johnny Dogs

10. Who phones up Campbell as a result of the article?
   a. David Lee
   b. Oswald Mosley
   c. Winston Churchill

11. What fate does Ada predict if the boys find out who's got her pregnant?
   a. Freddie will be cut into pieces
   b. Tommy will burn down the stables
   c. She will be sent to Australia

12. Grace is chatting with Tommy. Where does he say he wants to take her?
   a. To Dublin
   b. To London
   c. To the races

13. What name does Grace originally give Tommy in the cinema?
   a. Rudolph Valentino
   b. Harold Lloyd
   c. Rhys Mwyn

14. Polly's not impressed with Tommy fixing the race. What's his reply?
   a. The horse was nobbled before he could do anything
   b. Billy Kimber's there for the taking
   c. Billy Kimber's already working for Tommy

15. Where does Polly say she'll take Ada to get an abortion?
   a. Edinburgh
   b. Oswestry
   c. Cardiff

16. What gambit does Tommy open with Campbell?
   a. That he's a businessman and wants a successful business
   b. That Campbell simply should get out of Birmingham
   c. That what happened in France should stay there forever

17. And what does the Inspector say in return?
    a. That he wants a peacefully-run city
    b. That he has subdued Wales and will do the same to Tommy
    c. That there are no negotiations to be had

18. What deal gets agreed between the two?
    a. Campbell will leave, as soon as Tommy fixes up all the pubs
    b. Tommy will give Campbell the guns in return for the Specials leaving him and his business alone
    c. Tommy will not go out with Grace because he can see Campbell is in love with her

19. Curly convinces Tommy that the Lees have cursed the beautiful new horse. What does Tommy do?
    a. Shoots Curly and says he's a liar
    b. Shoots the horse, apologising to it first
    c. Sets the horse free in the marketplace

20. What does Tommy propose to Kimber?
    a. An alliance against the Lees
    b. An alliance against the Communists
    c. An alliance against the police

CILLIAN MURPHY

The hero of the piece – or the anti-hero depending on how you look at it – is the one and only Cillian Murphy. Handsome, charismatic, one of the masters of their art – these are things that are often said, but enough about the author of this quiz book, how much do we know about Tommy Shelby himself? Let's delve into his storied career outside the Blinders with a list of tricky questions…

1. Let's start with the happy day that Cillian was born. Do you know the day, month and year?
    a. 25 May 1976
    b. 7 June 1975
    c. 5 July 1967

2. What star sign does that make him?
    a. Gemini
    b. Taurus
    c. Sagittarius

3. In (a suburb of) which town, county/state and country was he born?
    a. Edinburgh, Dùn Èideann, Scotland
    b. Douglas, Cork, Ireland
    c. Toronto, Ontario, Canada

4. And in which Cork suburb did Cillian grow up?
    a. Ballykissangel
    b. Brianjones
    c. Ballintemple

5. In which religion was he raised?
    a. Jedi
    b. Catholic
    c. Presleytarian

6. Before making it big as a film star, Cillian was in various bands with his brothers. What was the name of his most famous group in his late teens and early twenties?
    a. Sons of Mr Green Genes
    b. Fathers of Sir Mighty Boog
    c. Sons and Daughters

7. They took their name from a song by which experimental jazz/pop/rock genius?
   a. Frank Zappa
   b. Vaffan Coulo
   c. Sultans of Ping FC

8. And what was Cillian's role in that band?
   a. Bassist and backing vocals
   b. Guitarist and singer
   c. Drummer and roadie

9. Which ultra-cool record label once offered them a deal?
   a. Factory
   b. Creation
   c. Acid Jazz

10. Cillian went to study while also playing in the band. Where did he go, and what subject did he read? A point for each.
   a. Dublin, acting
   b. Open University, sound technology
   c. Cork, law

11. While at university, he played the lead part at Cork Opera House in which horror-comedy?
   a. *Little Shop of Horrors*
   b. *Waiting for Godot*
   c. *Godzilla and the Pie Mystery*

12. What was his first professional stage job?
   a. A teenager in *Disco Pigs*
   b. A shoplifter in *Trainspotting*
   c. A zookeeper in *My Cousin's Bought a Zoo*

13. What was the name of the 2001 BBC mini-series Cillian was in, based on an Anthony Trollope novel of the same name?
   a. *Orley Farm*
   b. *The Three Clerks*
   c. *The Way We Live Now*

14. Cillian's movie breakthrough came in 2002 as the lead in a Danny Boyle post-apocalyptic piece. What was it called?
   a. *Threads*
   b. *Doctor Strangelove*
   c. *28 Days Later*

15. And what was the name of Cillian's character?
   a. Bill
   b. Jim
   c. Cranberry

16. What was the name of the 2003 movie in which Cillian plays a bored supermarket employee who plans a bank job?

a. *Interruption*
b. *Interrogation*
c. *Intermission*

17. What was the name of Cillian's villain in 2005's *Batman Begins*?

a. Dr. Crazylegs Crane
b. Sir Mix-a-Lot
c. Dr. Jonathan Crane

18. Which Palme d'Or-winning movie about the Irish Civil War and independence struggle did he appear in, in 2006?

a. *The Hand that Shakes the Cradle*
b. *The Wind in the Willows*
c. *The Wind that Shakes the Barley*

19. Cillian teamed up with Boyle again in 2007. What was that movie called?

a. *Nightsweat*
b. *Sunshine*
c. *Sunblest*

20. On which unusual format did Cillian's image appear, in July 2008? Hint: it set a lot of tongues wagging!

a. A postage stamp
b. A football sticker
c. An ice cream

21. In which sci-fi movie did he portray a businessman called Robert Fischer?

a. *Investment*
b. *Insincerity*
c. *Inception*

22. Which single-actor play, written and directed by Enda Walsh, did Cillian take from Galway to Brooklyn in 2011?

a. *Disco Pigs*
b. *Misterman*
c. *Postmanpat*

23. With which true cinema greats did he star in 2012's *Red Lights*?

a. Robert De Niro and Sigourney Weaver
b. Robert Del Naja and Banksy
c. Ian McShane and Nicholas Lyndhurst

24. What's the name of Cillian's radio show that he hosts on BBC 6 Music?

a. *Cillian Murphy's Hot Shots*

b. *Cillian's Cracking Tracks*

c. *Cillian Murphy's Limited Edition*

25. And for which mega-movie about nuclear bombs did Cillian's performance win many huge awards?

a. *Barbie*

b. *Oppenheimer*

c. *Einstein's Folly*

SERIES ONE:
EPISODE THREE

Thomas Shelby takes Grace to the races in Cheltenham... but little does she know that she's acting on different instructions other than a mere date. Tommy's also approached by some men sympathetic to a certain Irish cause. Meanwhile, Freddie and Ada are in an increasingly dangerous situation. The tense third episode really does barrel along with intrigue!

1. Those two strangers who meet Tommy at The Garrison offer decent money for the stash of guns. But who do they represent?
   a. The Lee family
   b. The Irish Republican Army
   c. The Kimber family

2. What colour does Tommy tell Grace to buy something in, and for what reason?
   a. Blue, to match Tommy's eyes
   b. Red, to match 'his' handkerchief
   c. Green, to match the verdant grass of Cheltenham

3. When the Sergeant tells Campbell that all his men served in the war (in France), what's Campbell's response?
   a. That France was easy for the plebs
   b. That he [Campbell] serves his country every day
   c. That he [Campbell] hates France

4. Grace scuffles with one of the IRA men, who says he's going to take her in for interrogation. But what happens?
   a. He accidentally gets shot to death
   b. She kicks him in the crotch and runs
   c. He's so drunk he falls in the canal

5. What does Campbell say happened, though?
   a. The man was drowned immediately
   b. There was no body, so no murder
   c. That the man was killed by his own people

6. To which country has Polly booked Ada and Freddie's 'permanent honeymoon'?
   a. Australia
   b. Germany
   c. America

7. Specifically, which city?
   a. Melbourne
   b. Cologne
   c. New York

8. What does Tommy say the Lees are planning to do at the races?
   a. Bet heavily on Morning Star, which Kimber plans to hobble so it can't win
   b. Get extremely drunk and refuse to pay their bar bill
   c. Lots of them will show up and rob the bookies

9. What's Freddie's question to the assembled crowd?
   a. Whether they are happy at work
   b. Whether they want to go on strike
   c. Whether they have a wedding gift for him

10. What's Tommy's unexpected gift to Arthur?
   a. A horse
   b. A car
   c. The pub

11. Tommy tells Freddie that the latter only wants a kid with Ada for the kudos of it. But Freddie says what?

   a. That he loves her and she loves him
   b. That he has no cause left anymore
   c. That France was nothing to do with it

12. Who unexpectedly turns up with news from London?

   a. Danny Whizz-Bang
   b. Freddie Thorne
   c. Winston Churchill

13. And what message does Tommy give him, to take back?

   a. That the IRA need to send someone up to talk
   b. That the IRA are finished in Birmingham
   c. That Oswald Mosley has no rights over the Blinders

14. Though he's great at working with motorcars, Charlie doesn't like them. Why?

   a. They're a new-fangled fad that won't last
   b. They've no heart – he can't talk with them
   c. They're dirty, smelly and too expensive

15. What does Arthur say has happened to Billy Kimber's men?
   a. That Kimber has forgotten to pay them so they're disloyal
   b. That Kimber has let them go rotten and they're on the take from the Lee family
   c. That Kimber will fight on the frontline and inspire them

16. What name does Tommy tell Grace she should tell security at the races?
   a. Lady Sarah Duggan
   b. Baroness Linda Robson
   c. Wilhelmina Fogg

17. What's the name of the man that the Blinders beat up in the toilet?
   a. Raz
   b. Ralph
   c. Bucko

18. How does Tommy get to sit down and negotiate with Billy Kimber?
   a. The Peaky Blinders have chased the Lees out of the races and retrieved all the stolen money
   b. Tommy reminds Billy that in France there was a mutual enemy against whom they both worked together
   c. He cuts Billy's ear off and feeds it to him

19. How much money does Tommy say he'll give Grace, who is to spend two hours with Kimber?
   a. £3
   b. £8
   c. Nothing

20. But what happens?
   a. Tommy goes to retrieve Grace, telling Kimber that she actually has syphilis
   b. Tommy takes the car home and tells Grace to walk back
   c. Kimber tells him he doesn't want any deal with the Blinders

SERIES ONE:
EPISODE FOUR

Tommy's growing profile has put him and the Shelbys firmly in the firing line, with the Lee family out for revenge. Will he be able to pacify the irate Lees? Concurrently, Inspector Campbell is keen to put Tommy under pressure about the guns, and the scenario is becoming personal. Grace gets closer to Arthur; Tommy makes another discovery about her; John finds something worrying out about Lizzie but who will he marry? Family, fighting, intrigue and even a baby born – what an episode!

1. Who is the only person left in the Shelby home when everyone goes for a meeting?
   a. Scudboat
   b. Motorhead
   c. Stripe

2. But who bursts in?
   a. The Lees
   b. The Kimbers
   c. Tommy, checking on him

3. Why does John specifically say he's getting married?
   a. He's not getting any younger
   b. The kids need a mother
   c. He's lonely and sad

4. In what situation does Polly say Lizzie's never done a day's work?
   a. Horizontal
   b. In the pub
   c. Vertical

5. What slightly baffling object have the Lees left at the Blinders' HQ?
   a. Half a pie
   b. Wire cutters
   c. Hairbrush

6. Why?
   a. It's to let the Shelbys know a hand grenade booby trap is nearby
   b. It's to show the Shelbys that they can't be 'cut off' so easily
   c. Because they've cut the wires, i.e. the telegraph to the police

7. Tommy manages to find the explosive device, and it goes off with nobody hurt after he chucks it away. What advice does he have for young Finn?
   a. Never go back to a lighted firework
   b. This is why Finn should not pretend to be Tommy
   c. Don't ever get into a fight you can't finish

8. What object does Tommy show Zilpha Lee at their sit-down?
   a. The pair of wire cutters
   b. A bullet with Tommy's name on it
   c. A newspaper article about the Blinders

9. What bombshell does Tommy pull out when she asks why she should trust him?
   a. That he knows she's undercover police
   b. That he's kin on his mother's side
   c. That he's confirmed the deal with Kimber

10. Whose address is in the envelope?
   a. Danny Whizz-Bang
   b. Second Prize Steve
   c. Stanley Chapman

11. Tommy gives it to Campbell, on what condition?
   a. That the Inspector lets Freddie and Ada leave Birmingham
   b. That the Inspector never tells anyone where he got it
   c. That the Inspector looks into the background of Lizzie

12. What does Campbell warn Tommy in return?
   a. That if the guns aren't handed over before Campbell is replaced, all hell will break loose
   b. That if Freddie and Ada are still in Birmingham by sunset, the police will arrest them
   c. That if Tommy doesn't straighten out his ideas, he'll be dead soon

13. But why does Freddie not worry about Chapman being arrested?
   a. Chapman doesn't know Freddie's address
   b. Chapman is a small part of the bigger picture
   c. Chapman is working with the Lees

14. What is the gift which Billy Kimber hands to Tommy?
    a. A legitimate betting licence
    b. A palomino horse in great condition
    c. A winning betting slip

15. What are Tommy's orders about contraband?
    a. Never leave it alone after dark
    b. Keep it near petrol boat moorings
    c. Keep the rats away from it

16. What job does Tommy offer Grace?
    a. Head barmaid at the pub
    b. Second in command
    c. Bookkeeper

17. How is he sure that Grace is Protestant rather than Catholic?
    a. She doesn't cross herself in the church
    b. She doesn't wear a cross on a necklace
    c. She doesn't wear Catholic boots

18. How much money does Lizzie accept from Tommy?
    a. £10
    b. £8
    c. £2

19. Tommy says the war with the Lees will be finished once and for all. How?

  a. The Shelbys wipe them all out with a machine gun
  b. The Lees agree to leave Birmingham forever
  c. John is to be married to a Lee girl called Esme

20. Ada gives birth to a boy and Freddie manages to get to see him! But – what happens?

  a. Ada tells him it's Tommy's son
  b. The police burst in and arrest Freddie
  c. Polly won't let him in the house

CHAIN SPELLERS

Reckon you can spell? Okey dokey – let's find out!

Players: Two or more

You Will Need: Nothing except a knowledge of the alphabet – and the TV show! A pencil and paper is handy to keep score, as ever.

How to Play: Team One is spellers, and the other will be guessers. Team One has 10 seconds to prepare a word, and may confer if there are multiple players on the team. They then start (slowly) spelling a word or phrase related to *Peaky Blinders*, and Team Two must guess it as quickly as possible! If you guess correctly, you get a point. If you guess incorrectly, the spelling team gets a point. Swap over after each word or phrase so that everyone gets a chance to both spell and guess. First to 10 points is the winner.

Variation One: The guessing team has three lives – and can keep guessing until all three lives are lost. If a guess is correct, they gain a point, and if they guess incorrectly, a life is lost. Repeat until all three lives are lost, and then swap over guessers with spellers. Whichever team ends up with the most points is the winner. Note that here the teams stay as they are until three lives are up, and the aim of the game is to accumulate as high a score as possible.

Variation Two: Points per letter. As soon as a correct guess is made, count the letters which are remaining in the word or phrase and award them to the guessing team. If the guess is incorrect, those points are awarded to the spelling team. Swap over after each word or phrase – if the guessers don't know the answer at the end of the word or phrase, the spellers get a bonus point.

Variation Three: Before starting the game, give each team a two-minute preparation time to decide which words or phrases they're going to use. The teams may write these down but obviously do not share them with the guessers. If you are playing a version of the game that involves swapping over after each guess, then clearly there will be some words that are on both teams' sheet. When you are on a guessing team you *may not* look at your words list! No cheating now!

Variation Four: One player is the spellmeister and everyone else must guess. A free-for-all will ensue! Keep score – the guesser with the most points is the winner – and unlimited unpunished guesses apply.

You could also make it knockout so that any unsuccessful guess puts that player out of the game. Last person standing wins.

If nobody hazards a guess at all, then the speller is the winner – so there's no advantage for sitting back and letting everyone else self-destruct with incorrect guesses.

Note: You can have one challenge each. That is, if you feel the word or phrase is too obscure or not appropriate to the show, you can hold up your hand and request that the other players adjudicate on the validity of the speller's offering. If the adjudication ends in deadlock, the word stands. There's no punishment for an unsuccessful challenge, but a successful one wipes out all the scores and any unsuccessful challengers are back in. The speller must begin the round again with a different word or phrase. Once a player has invoked their single challenge, they cannot challenge again.

SERIES ONE: EPISODE FIVE

Those guns which had everyone in a tizzy are back in play, with the IRA back on the scene, meaning we've got more of that Tommy–Inspector Campbell shaky relationship to entertain us. But where do Grace's loyalties really lie? Campbell tries to make sure her considerable talents as an operative remain as close to home as possible. Yes, as the series begins to wind towards its conclusion there are many threads spinning all at once. Which ones will snap under the tension?

1. Who does Tommy say did not shop Freddie Thorne to the police?
   a. Arthur
   b. Tommy himself
   c. Grace

2. What colour star does Tommy use to designate the day that Billy Kimber will be taken down?
   a. Yellow
   b. Blue
   c. Black

3. And on which date does he draw that star? Proper blink-and-you'll-miss-it one this!
   a. 3 December
   b. 5 November
   c. 26 October

4. Who do we find out is running the boxing ring?
   a. Marston
   b. King
   c. Hofmeister

5. But Mr Marston tells who to shove his licence up his arse crack?
   a. Tommy
   b. Arthur
   c. John

6. In fact, that name's shouted out for us. By whom?
   a. Tommy's dad
   b. Arthur's dad
   c. John's dad

7. Whose real name do we find out is actually Daniel Owen?

   a. Billy Kimber
   b. Danny Whizz-Bang
   c. Finn Shelby

8. Arthur Snr says he's seen the light in America. What money-raising idea does he have?

   a. Motor racing
   b. Horseracing
   c. Casinos

9. What's the full name of the Irish man who comes to see Tommy?

   a. Martin Ross
   b. Matthew Brady
   c. Malacki Byrne

10. When does Arthur Snr tell Arthur Jnr that they will set sail for the USA?

   a. Thursday
   b. Saturday
   c. Friday

11. Tommy knows he's going to be ambushed at midnight – but by the peals of the bells of which church?
   a. St Andrew's
   b. St James'
   c. St John's

12. On which bell toll were the police meant to enter the room?
   a. The first
   b. The last
   c. The sixth

13. In Sergeant Moss's report to Campbell, what were Grace and Tommy doing when the police came in?
   a. Fighting
   b. Drinking
   c. Embracing

14. Why does Grace tell Campbell that her reasons for joining the service have now gone?
   a. Because her need to avenge her father is no longer there
   b. Because Campbell is too overbearing as a boss
   c. Because now she is far enough away from Ireland

15. What does Grace demand from Campbell if she tells him where the guns are?
    a. To not harm Tommy
    b. To go away immediately
    c. To give them to the IRA

16. And where have the guns been all along?
    a. In the walls of the warehouse
    b. In Danny Whizz-Bang's grave
    c. In a secret room of the pub

17. How did they keep the guns from getting damp?
    a. Lined the grave with lead
    b. Wrapped them up in cloth
    c. Dismantled them

18. Unexpectedly, what does Campbell ask of Grace?
    a. If she will take over his spot as inspector
    b. If she will be his wife
    c. If she will kill Tommy

19. What does Arthur Jnr have printed on his new business cards?
    a. Arthur Shelby: Associate Bookmaker
    b. Arthur Shelby: Peaky Blinder
    c. Arthur Shelby: Don't Mess With the Best

20. Who are the three shareholders in that business?
    a. Arthur Jnr, Arthur Snr and Polly
    b. Grace, Polly and Ada
    c. Arthur Jnr, Tommy and John

SERIES ONE:
EPISODE SIX

It's crunch time for everyone; Billy Kimber's fate approaches, while the rebuffed Inspector Campbell's grudge against Tommy and the Blinders has become an obsession. He has a plan to rid Small Heath of the various gangs, but how will it fare? Will he be able to change Grace's mind so she will marry him? Or will he come to a grisly end himself? It's all-action in the season finale.

1. We see a man in the Chinese place who exits as Campbell enters. What is that man doing?
   a. Making a sandwich
   b. Brushing his teeth
   c. Cutting cloth

2. Who do we see praying for the Shelby boys?
   a. Grace
   b. Ada
   c. Polly

3. With whom does Campbell have a meeting at midday?
   a. Oswald Mosley
   b. Winston Churchill
   c. Carlton Wuck

4. Campbell tells Tommy that men like them will always be alone. What's Tommy's response?
   a. That Tommy has his family
   b. That Campbell has the police
   c. That loners always win

5. Why did the police take away Polly's two children?
   a. The police found a gin-making apparatus
   b. The police were rounding up Shelbys
   c. The police saw the kids were not in church

6. What association does Tommy say the Blinders will join that day?
   a. The National Horseracing Syndicate
   b. The National Association of Racecourse Bookmakers
   c. The National Club for Birmingham Horse Owners

7. At which race venue is the big event to take place?
   a. Worcester races
   b. Kempton races
   c. Bangor races

8. Who does the officer say told him to volunteer to accompany Freddie in the van?
   a. The Lees
   b. The Peaky Blinders
   c. Inspector Campbell

9. Who brings the bad news that the Kimber boys are actually headed to intercept the Blinders?
   a. Inspector Campbell
   b. Jimmy Jesus
   c. Robert Devil

10. Why does Polly say that she and Grace are drinking rather than fighting (other than they have more sense than that)?
   a. The Blinders owe Grace, for saving Tommy's life
   b. Polly says it'd be too easy to take out a little girl like Grace
   c. Because Campbell is lurking outside, waiting to come in

11. What did Tommy want to do, before the war changed everything and everyone?
   a. Work with horses
   b. Work with steel
   c. Own a pub

12. As far as Polly's concerned, Grace is a … what?
   a. A no-good twopenny whore
   b. An Irish liar and thief
   c. A snitch from the Parish

13. By how much are the Blinders outnumbered?
   a. Two to one
   b. Three to one
   c. Ten to one

14. Tommy doesn't call his troops Peaky Blinders – by which wartime name does he call them?
   a. The Small Heath Rifles
   b. The Birmingham Platoon
   c. The Birmingham Bastard Squad

15. The news comes to Campbell that there are men heading up and there will be a big fight. What surprising orders does he give to the police, and why?
   a. To stand down and let the gangs wipe each other out
   b. To go home and start praying that it's over quickly
   c. To tool up on any household knives they can find

16. Tommy says neither the past nor the future is his concern. Which three-word reply does he give when asked what his concern actually is?
    a. Small Heath Rifles
    b. The one minute
    c. The next minute

17. Sergeant Moss is disgusted with Campbell for what he reckons is looking the other way. But Campbell replies vigorously – what does he say?
    a. That he has never looked the other way in his life and won't start now
    b. That Sergeant Moss is part of the problem for being so weak
    c. That he, Campbell, is looking directly at what's transpiring, and he likes it

18. Who gets, literally, between the two gangs as they're about to shoot the hell out of each other?
    a. Ada and the new baby
    b. Polly and Arthur Snr
    c. Campbell and Churchill

19. But Kimber does something underhand, then Tommy steps in and ends it, how?
   a. Kimber shoots Danny Whizz-Bang dead; Tommy shoots Kimber in the head and tells the Kimbers to go home to their families – it's over
   b. Kimber takes hold of Ada and uses her as a human shield before shooting Polly; Tommy takes Polly's hand and tells her that it's all finished
   c. Kimber shoots Jimmy Jesus through the heart and tells him that God is dead; Tommy says he never believed and there's no heaven and hell for anyone

20. The Shelbys are now the third-largest legal bookmakers at a racetrack in the country. Which two families are ahead of them?
   a. The Lees and the Garrisons
   b. The Sabinis and the Solomons
   c. The Solomons and the Campbells

SERIES ONE: SOUNDTRACK

Any legendary TV show worth its salt must have a bangin' soundtrack to go alongside the brilliant visuals, the stunning acting and of course the wonderful writing. Here, we've gone through each series and noted the songs that helped to make the episodes so memorable. How well do you know the soundtrack to Peaky Blinders*? Let's have a crack…*

1. If you don't know this then we're not sure we can be pals. What's the name of the title music for the show?
    a. 'Red Right Hand'
    b. 'Blue Balls'
    c. 'Pain And Glory'

2. And which gothy superstar band is responsible?
    a. Nick Drake and the Gravelax
    b. Nick Cave and the Bad Seeds
    c. The Birthday Party

3. The same individual also has several tracks in Series One, alongside his long-time collaborator and fiddle player extraordinaire. What's the violinist and multi-instrumentalist's name?
   a. Wayne County
   b. Warren Peace
   c. Warren Ellis

4. A punk/rock and roll superstar and his sister (or wife) are also regulars on the soundtrack. But what's that duo called?
   a. Royal Blood
   b. Thompson Twins
   c. White Stripes

5. And what is the guitarist/singer/frontman's name?
   a. Jack Black
   b. Jack White
   c. Jackson Browne

6. Which song, originally by U2, do we hear the frontman cover?
   a. 'Angel of Harlem'
   b. 'Love is Blindness'
   c. 'Where the Streets Have No Name'

7. That version became the title music for a 2024 series. Which one?
   a. *The Agency*
   b. *The Madness*
   c. *The Penguin*

8. Which growly voiced bluesy rocker do we hear singing the song 'Clap Hands'?
   a. Tom Kincaid
   b. Tom Petty
   c. Tom Waits

9. And which musician presents us with 'The Prowl'?
   a. Dan Auerbach
   b. Daniel Johnston
   c. Michael Johnston

10. What's the name of that chap's main band?
   a. The Blue Meanies
   b. The Black Keys
   c. Back in Black

WASN'T SHE IN...?

Players: Unlimited

How to Play: This one requires the agreement of all players *beforehand* otherwise it's gonna get very messy. You will need to nominate a quizmeister, who in this case must be in charge of the remote control, and also nominate a reference book/website such as IMDB, which has details of which shows any actor/actress has appeared in, and gained a named credit.

All players watch *Peaky Blinders* – a random episode if you like – until, at a random point as chosen by the quizmeister, the programme is paused to show just one character. The quizmeister then asks: '*What else was s/he in?*'. All the other players must then bid a number, which indicates how many other programmes/films/plays *that they can name* in which the actor that played that particular character appeared. The highest bidder must then name all those shows. A point for each!

However, if the player cannot name that number of shows, then they gain no points and the player that claimed the second-highest amount steps in to complete their own, lower number. Note that you can name the same shows as the first player! If the second player cannot complete this task, then the player in third place is in the hotseat up to the number they claimed they could identify.

Points *only* to the person who completes their task. All answers must be checked against the agreed database.

Variation One: Appearances as an unnamed extra are also allowed – but the player identifying them must find a screenshot of the actor to back up their claim.

Variation Two: *She wasn't actually in that*. If you can name a show that everyone else thinks said actress/actor was in, but this is an urban myth or simply not true, then you gain an extra point.

Variation Three: Allow all appearances on chat shows – this one's going to take a *lot* of checking, though, and the player must again find the clip in question. Use a time limit here cause it'll take hours otherwise!

Variation Four: Use only appearances on one format. That is, only radio shows count; only movies released at the cinema count; only straight-to-TV movies count, etc. Be brutal!

As you can imagine, this game is all about waiting for the quizmeister to pause the episode – so no complaining from players who've got completely engrossed in the programme, please. (Or, at least, no swearing.)

SERIES TWO

SERIES TWO:
EPISODE ONE

Two years have gone by in Blinders-land and we still don't know the fate of Grace and/or Inspector Campbell. Will we find out the significance of that gunshot? And how is Tommy feeling? Alone, as Campbell once told him he'd always be? Or has he moved on? Eyes look towards business in London, though one experienced family member urges caution on that front. Meanwhile, there's a sad death in the family, and that's where we can pick up the thread...

1. Whose funeral is it at which the family has gathered?
   a. Arthur Snr
   b. Freddie Thorne
   c. Danny Whizz-Bang

2. Tommy survived the hell of the Great War, but what was it that did for him?
   a. Pestilence
   b. Fire
   c. Drowning

3. How many cars does Tommy have, and of what make? Two points on offer here.
   a. Six; Rolls-Royce
   b. None; all destroyed
   c. Four; Bugatti

4. Why does Tommy tell Ada it's going to be dangerous to be a Shelby in London?
   a. Business expansion
   b. Revenge for Freddie
   c. Police corruption

5. According to the officer in charge, at what time did The Garrison blow up?
   a. Exactly 7am
   b. Approximately 9am
   c. Dead-on midnight

6. Tommy heads to the Black Lion, but where is Arthur and why?

   a. At Worcester races, fixing the odds
   b. At The Garrison, making sure the whisky isn't stolen by police
   c. Gone to visit Lizzie so she can take his mind off things

7. Why does Irene O'Donnell say that Tommy has been chosen?

   a. Because he's the calmest man under pressure
   b. Because he's got the manpower and the willpower
   c. Because he researches his enemies

8. A certain Inspector Campbell reappears… but what's his new rank?

   a. Rear gunner
   b. Major
   c. Sergeant at Arms

9. The Governor, in a classic expositional speech, says that the man in the cells was told there would be a pardon at the last minute. The person who told him was a chief of staff in intelligence, from Ulster, who carries … what … due to … what?

   a. A cane with a wolf-head handle; a bullet wound in his right leg

b. A leather attaché case; inside information on everyone
c. A sword with a wolf insignia; a stab wound in his heart

10. In the past year, how much has the Blinders operation been making per day?
a. £150
b. £2
c. £100

11. Esme speaks up. She has kin in London – whereabouts?
a. Wembley and the South Bank
b. The City and Cockfosters
c. Shepherd's Bush and Portobello

12. All the London bosses will be at Newmarket. But who has been at war for six months?
a. Italian and Jewish gangs
b. Italian and German soldiers
c. Irish and Scottish expats

13. Where do we surprisingly see Polly?
a. In London
b. At a spiritualist (medium)
c. At the shoe store

14. Is it good news for her?
  a. Yes
  b. No

15. In the bar, there's some crazy-ass music playing. What genre?
  a. Heavy metal
  b. Jazz
  c. Sputnik

16. Tommy makes his accustomed speech – what does he say the Blinders came to London for?
  a. To make new friends – those who were last will soon be first
  b. To kick some Southern arse – there's a new boss in town
  c. To have a holiday – no violence this weekend

17. Campbell walks into Churchill's office – but is confronted by what exactly?
  a. A rabid dog straining at the leash
  b. A nude woman modelling for Churchill
  c. Two bald men fighting in a sack

18. That shock over, what do we find out from the men's conversation?
   a. That Campbell is keen to go to Birmingham and burn it down
   b. That Campbell intends to use Tommy as an agent
   c. That Campbell distrusts Churchill and threatens him

19. Tommy goes back to see Lizzie – and what happens?
   a. The two end up in bed as usual, and Tommy pays her double
   b. Tommy offers her a job as a secretary in the business
   c. Tommy tells her to get out of Birmingham and stay away from him

20. Sabini and his boys give Tommy an absolute kicking – he's going to die because he's taken the side of the Jewish gang. But which unlikely person saves him and Lizzie?
   a. Freddie Thorne
   b. Danny Whizz-Bang
   c. Major Campbell

SERIES TWO: EPISODE TWO

Campbell goes to visit Tommy, who's convalescing in the hospital; the latter later takes a slow boat to London, where he meets up with the Jewish gang's leader for the first time. He's also been recruited for a special job and uses his leverage to petition Churchill himself. Arthur, however, is suffering badly, with terrible consequences – until young Finn brings him a new 'medication' that seems to bring energy and positivity back. Polly gets some male attention, first physically, and then involving someone special from her past.

1. For whose murder does Campbell say he knows Tommy is responsible?
   a. Eamonn Duggan
   b. Eamonn Hughes
   c. Eamonn Andrews

2. We find out from both Campbell and Tommy where Grace is, and her situation. Explain both.
   a. She's in Poughkeepsie, New York, and married to a rich banker
   b. She's in London and hanging around with the Jewish gang
   c. She's succumbed to the Spanish Flu and has died

3. Campbell says he'll be back in touch with Tommy – when?
   a. As the midnight clock strikes six times
   b. When Tommy can piss standing up
   c. When Campbell decides to and not before

4. How long will it take for the boat to get to London?
   a. A month
   b. A day
   c. Four days

5. What three essential goods does Curly have for the trip?
   a. Magazines, beer and cheese
   b. Plasters, bandages and liniment
   c. Tobacco, tea and whisky

6. How many loaves does Alfie tell Tommy that the bakery produces weekly?
   a. Over a thousand
   b. Over a hundred
   c. Over ten thousand

7. What offensive stereotype does Alfie invoke regarding the way Tommy looks?
   a. That he'd have a big gold ring through his nose
   b. That he'd be selling lucky heather
   c. That he'd be telling his fortune

8. What does Tommy gift Ada?
   a. A house
   b. A flat
   c. A boat

9. Why does Mr Sabini get incredibly angry?
   a. He thinks the police have done a deal with Tommy
   b. He thinks the police have burnt down the Jewish bakery
   c. His subordinate has failed to tell him the police arrived

10. In Polly's new house, she and Tommy have a conversation. What does he say he wants to do?
   a. Use various contacts to track down Campbell and murder him
   b. Use various contacts to get some intelligence on Churchill
   c. Use various contacts to try and track down Polly's kids

11. Why is everything in The Garrison green?
   a. Arthur forgot to pay the decorators and pulled out a gun
   b. Arthur said it was a calming colour to do business
   c. The paint came from a railway warehouse

12. To whom does Tommy dictate a letter?
   a. Campbell
   b. Churchill
   c. Sabini

13. And what does Tommy ask for?
   a. An immediate cessation to all activities
   b. An export licence to various parts of the world
   c. An import licence for firearms

14. Tommy goes to visit a Mrs Johnson. Why?
    a. Her adopted son, Henry, is Polly's lad
    b. Her husband, Harry, is a Jewish gangster
    c. Her cousin, Alfie, is head baker

15. Finn's busy sparring – not too successfully – but his uncle Arthur is concurrently doing what?
    a. Smoking a massive opium pipe and lazing around
    b. Smuggling guns to the IRA
    c. Beating someone to death in a frenzy

16. What's in the sandwich that Moss and Campbell talk about?
    a. Sausage and pickle, with a soupçon of butter
    b. Tongue and pickle, with a stroke of mustard
    c. Beef and onion, with a splatter of tomato

17. What was the fate of Anna?
    a. She was placed with a family of acrobats from South Wales but died in a trapeze accident
    b. She was placed with a family of horse riders from the United States but died from being trampled
    c. She was placed with the family of a Stafford stationmaster, sent to Australia and died from spring fever

18. What does young Finn give to Arthur, to get him to come to the pub reopening?
   a. A letter from America
   b. Some 'Tokyo' to perk him up
   c. Some whisky from a special bottle

19. Polly won't talk to Tommy until she has … what?
   a. Some Tokyo
   b. A tugboat ticket
   c. An address

20. Which name does Henry give when he says he's looking for someone?
   a. Thomas Shelby
   b. Elizabeth Gray
   c. Eritrea Mountebank

SAM NEILL

The hard-ass nemesis of the Shelbys, and love rival to Thomas. But Campbell's strengths are also weaknesses, and ultimately his time in Birmingham is at best a mixed bag. But how about the actor who plays him? There's a brilliant career to talk about...

1. What's Sam Neill's full name?
   a. Samuel Van der Zil Neill
   b. Nigel Howard Adkins Neill
   c. Nigel John Dermot Neill

2. And where was he born?
   a. New Zealand
   b. Wales
   c. Northern Ireland

3. What nationality is he?
   a. New Zealander
   b. German
   c. Australian

4. Sam is an extremely well-decorated person. Can you name his three most prestigious titles? Clue: he has many acting awards, but these are not awarded by that industry – think national honours.
   a. OBE, KNZM, Knighthood
   b. CBE, Baronhood, WFH
   c. MBE, QVC, DVD

5. What's the name of the 1977 New Zealand movie in which he made his international mark?
   a. *Breathing Slowly*
   b. *Sleeping Dogs*
   c. *Smiling Politely*

6. Sam starred opposite Judy Davis in which 1979 success?
   a. *My Brilliant Career*
   b. *My Favourite Laundrette*
   c. *My Greatest Moment*

7. What was the full name of the *Omen* movie in which Sam played the son of the Devil?

a. *The Omen: Devil Takes His Due*

b. *Omen IV: Intravenous Evil*

c. *Omen III: The Final Conflict*

8. And what is his character's name in that movie?

a. Darren Bettis

b. Damien Thorn

c. Dermot Killer

9. In which historical drama did Sam play Cardinal Thomas Wolsey?

a. *The Owains*

b. *The Tudors*

c. *The Joneses*

10. What was the name of the 2015 BBC TV series in which Sam played General MacArthur?

a. *Take It To The Limit*

b. *Three Little Indians*

c. *And Then There Were None*

11. By which author was the original thriller that the series was based on?

a. Ben Aaranovich

b. Ben Myers

c. Agatha Christie

12. What's the name of his recurring character in the *Jurassic Park* franchise?
   a. Dr Alan Bennett
   b. Dr Alan Grant
   c. Dr Grant Mitchell

13. Sam plays Brett Colby in this recent legal drama series. Can you name the series?
   a. *The Twelve*
   b. *Ocean's Eleven*
   c. *Three Times a Lady*

14. In 2023, he released his autobiography. But what was it called?
   a. *Did I Ever Tell You This? A Memoir*
   b. *Jurassic Neill: Be A DO-Ceratops*
   c. *Bring On The Empty Horses*

15. What is the name of Sam's winery?
   a. One More For The Road
   b. Two Paddocks
   c. Three Fellows Wanted

16. How many times has he been married?
   a. Once
   b. Twice
   c. Thrice

17. And how many children does he have?
    a. Four
    b. Three
    c. Two

18. Sam plays a detective in *Peaky Blinders*. Which subject did he initially – unsuccessfully – study at the University of Canterbury?
    a. Policing
    b. Bootlegging
    c. Law

19. Why is he known as Sam, rather than Nigel?
    a. He and his best friend Nigel Nut decided to call themselves cowboy-type names at school. Nigel Nut became Bill, and Nigel Neill became Sam
    b. When he was a young man his nephew had huge trouble pronouncing 'Nigel' and instead referred to him as 'Uncle Sam'
    c. When he was applying to get an Equity card there was already a Nigel Neill out there working so he had to pick a different name at random

20. Sam has been undergoing chemotherapy since March 2022 for what kind of blood cancer?
    a. Angioimmunoblastic T-cell Lymphoma
    b. Bovine Spongiform Encephalopathy
    c. Pyroclastic Flow Pooling

SERIES TWO:
EPISODE THREE

You lookin' for trouble? You've come to the right place. The big question is whether Tommy Shelby is biting off more than he can chew by trying his luck in taking on the London big sharks. Arthur is facing consequences for losing control of himself (not for the first time, it must be said), and the newest member of the Shelby clan brings a sense of calm eloquence to matters – undercut no doubt by hidden depths of potential violence. Business as usual!

1. What does Campbell say the King has offered to the rebel Irish?
    a. A treaty
    b. A war
    c. An audience

2. Who wants to accept it, but who does not?
    a. The IRA wants to accept, but the Fenians (Protestants) do not
    b. The Fenians (Protestants) want to accept, but the IRA does not

3. Because the new generation of kids hasn't been to war and fought, Tommy remarks, they...?
    a. Are soft
    b. Can't shoot
    c. Stay kids

4. What kind of horse does Michael say he has?
    a. A palomino stud
    b. A white shire horse
    c. A Grey mare

5. He was Corporal Billy Kitchen, but working for the Blinders what rank does he have?
    a. Lieutenant Kitchen
    b. Brigadier Kitchen
    c. Captain Kitchen

6. And how many men will he be in charge of?
    a. 10
    b. 100
    c. 60

7. Michael says if he has to spend one more day in the village, he'll do what?
   a. Go completely insane and jump in the river
   b. Go to church and confess all the Blinders' sins
   c. Blow up the village's wishing well with dynamite

8. What's the name of the baking company into which many men enrol?
   a. Camden's Best Bread
   b. The Aerated Bread Company of Camden Town
   c. Kingsmill and Sons, Bread of Distinctive Taste

9. What do Rule No. 1 and Rule No. 2 have in common, as explained by Alfie Solomons?
   a. They are not to be discussed
   b. There are no rules in Camden
   c. Employees Must Wash Hands

10. Arthur opens the pub, but who is the first person through that door?
   a. The mother of the lad he battered to death in the boxing ring
   b. The sister of the woman he made pregnant and forced to have an abortion
   c. Major Campbell and a phalanx of his best Specials

11. Charlie's not happy. How much more per boat does he want?

   a. A pound
   b. Ten shillings
   c. Tree fiddy

12. Who does Major Campbell have a picture of, in his wallet?

   a. Winston Churchill
   b. Grace Burgess
   c. Polly Shelby

13. What did Campbell's new landlady previously do, according to Tommy?

   a. Run a terrible chophouse in Aigburth
   b. Run a famous brothel in Stechford
   c. Run an insanitary canteen in Romford

14. Who have the police arrested?

   a. Harry Hancox, aka The Digbeth Kid
   b. Barry Balloon, aka The Big Chopper
   c. Jimmy Jackson, aka The Righteous Man

15. What happens to him?

   a. Sabini has him killed
   b. He escapes on a palomino mare
   c. He slips past the police and runs

16. What are the unfortunate lad's parting words?
    a. 'I'm not real'
    b. 'I'm a copper'
    c. 'I'm your kin'

17. Why does Tommy want to spend a fortune on a horse?
    a. To win races for a change as he loves horses
    b. To make sure he can get around if his car breaks down
    c. To gain access to the owners' enclosure

18. How did Michael's dad die?
    a. Drunk, between a boat and a lock
    b. In the war, shot in the throat
    c. In a backroom bar fight over horses

19. After buying the horse, who does Tommy meet?
    a. May Carleton, a breeder and trainer
    b. Betty Crockett, a baker and firelighter
    c. Mary Beckett, a mother and crofter

20. How does Michael describe his kin to Polly when he comes home?
    a. They were total dudes
    b. They were really amazing
    c. They were a bunch of thugs

SERIES TWO: EPISODE FOUR

The Blinders make inroads into London, starting with a club of their very own, though their methods are typically – shall we say – unconventional. The Byzantine nature of shifting gang alliances once more puts Tommy et al. in the centre of some tricky ground, however. The Blinders' leader is also given another task to do by his reluctant co-conspirator, Major Campbell. It's also the coming-of-age time for the new lad, who starts to really see the darkness the Peaky Blinders are capable of.

1. In the meeting with Campbell et al., Tommy spits out a splendid line. He says he's there to listen, but not to…?

   a. Idiot coppers
   b. Irish bastards
   c. The infantry

2. What is Tommy's revelation about Donal Henry?
   a. Donal is a spy
   b. Donal is not Irish
   c. Donal is a copper

3. And what does Tommy say has to happen before he takes the assignment?
   a. Campbell resigns
   b. Donal has to die
   c. Donal must go to Ireland

4. What iconic phrase does Arthur gleefully recite into the microphone?
   a. 'By order of the Peaky Blinders'
   b. 'Youse are all fucking finished'
   c. 'Snitches get stitches'

5. What job does Michael ask Tommy for?
   a. Chief bottlewasher at The Garrison
   b. Accounts clerk
   c. Dispersal officer

6. Where does Esme say she slept when she was a baby?
   a. In a haystack
   b. In a manger
   c. In the stables

7. May says she thought she was going to get murdered when she drove into Small Heath, but when she mentioned Tommy's name, how did she then get treated?

a. Even worse, so she's lucky to be alive
b. With the utter indifference of a pagan
c. Like being escorted to a king

8. What time will the horsebox be leaving?

a. 1pm
b. 2pm
c. Midday

9. What does May drink in the pub?

a. Gin with cordial
b. Whisky with soda
c. Rum and water

10. To what do they drink?

a. To Peaky Blinders
b. To The Derby
c. To the police

11. What is the name of Tommy's horse?

a. Carleton Wuck
b. Campbell's Soup
c. Grace's Secret

12. To protect Michael, what does Tommy promise Polly?
    a. That Michael will only be in charge of new business
    b. That Michael will be blindfolded and driven to work
    c. That Michael will never have to meet Alfie Solomon

13. What does Tommy give Michael as a birthday gift, so the latter is never late for work?
    a. A calendar with his picture on it
    b. A golden pocket watch
    c. A Swiss Army wristwatch

14. What is the export crate marked up as, and where is it headed?
    a. Riley car spares, for Halifax, Nova Scotia
    b. Peaked caps, for Los Angeles
    c. Racehorse hair, for Wales

15. How many bottles of whisky will be hidden within those crates?
    a. 500
    b. 50
    c. 10

16. How much has been taken on 'olives'?
   a. £600
   b. £60
   c. £6

17. If Arthur doesn't straighten up, what will Tommy do?
   a. Give the place back to the Italians
   b. Bring in Alfie to kick some heads in
   c. Replace Arthur with John

18. How long does it take for Tommy's car to be noticed by police?
   a. About 10 minutes
   b. 23 seconds
   c. 69 seconds

19. Trouble is brewing (surprise, surprise). What is eventually sorted between the Solomons' gang and the Italians?
   a. They will never step on each other's toes
   b. They will unite against the Shelbys
   c. They will diversify into pie making

20. Michael is in the pub with his mate, both smoking and drinking, but Paddy isn't happy about it. Why?
   a. Paddy doesn't like the Shelbys
   b. Paddy hates Black people
   c. Paddy doesn't want to smoke

SPEAKY BLINDERS

Peaky Blinders *is a show that is meticulous about getting everything lined up, so it can be incredibly resonant of a time and place. The sets, the lighting, the clothes are all extensively researched to be historically accurate – and the language that the characters speak is no exception.*

The Shelby family's origins are both Romani and Irish Traveller, so their lexicon draws from both plus local Birmingham slang of the time. (It has also been noted that in the first couple of series, the language was Romanian rather than Romani – a mistake corrected thereafter.)

Now as it happens humans are pretty good at getting the gist of a sentence even if we don't know exactly what every single word individually means, but let's get right into the nitty-gritty with the meanings of some of the words and phrases we've encountered over the course of the show.

Match the word with the definition:

WORD	DEFINITION
Peaky	Pregnant
Blinder	Those who write odds on the bookie's chalk boards, and those who write the betting slips
Snow	Bookmaker
Up the duff	Sexually transmitted disease, generally syphilis
The clap	A scheduled discussion, particularly between rivals
Bookie	A flat cap with a peak
Chalkers and rafflers	A kind of World War I PTSD, known after World War II as 'shell shock'
The cut	Stylish, dapper, generally great/ Member of a gang that takes eyes
Flanders blues	Canal
Parley	Cocaine

Over to you: Which other slang words have you picked up from the show? Are they suitable for sharing in polite company? Or impolite company? Share them with your friends and family – you have our permission, so show them this part of the book. Note that any offence taken on their part is not our responsibility though. We're innocent and naive little angels who have no idea what any of those words mean, capiche? Here are a couple of ideas of games you can play…

Local slang: What are the local words you like the most? Perhaps you've heard a new way to say someone's with child, or that they're a wrong 'un (i.e. someone naughty)? What words and phrases are your favourites? Go around the room and ask everybody to provide a slang word which everyone else must guess the meaning to. Which word was the funniest/best/made everybody make a shocked face?

Slip it in: Steady now – this game merely means that your task for the evening is to slip into conversation a slang word that you've invented. Will you be able to get everyone saying 'slads' by the end of the evening, to describe a sandwich?

Or, if someone's stubbed their toe, will you be able to convince them that where you grew up the correct word is 'finglestrap'? You might just start a new linguistic craze, and eventually end up on BBC Radio Two with a six-part series travelling around searching for the etymological source of all curse words. If, and when you do, we're in for 10 per cent of the fee as per usual. Hey, this is a *Peaky Blinders* book – we're simply joining in with the spirit of the show!

SERIES TWO: EPISODE FIVE

London bites back and bites back hard as the Peaky Blinders suddenly find themselves outflanked and out-thought. Arthur takes a break from being a crazed violent lunatic to find himself put in the frame even though on this occasion he's actually innocent. But what does Major Campbell have to do with all this? Tommy's head is turned by a phone call; Polly has to sacrifice something for her son; and there's a bona fide Hollywood superstar moment, too. What an episode!

1. To which Jewish festival has Alfie invited Arthur and Billy Kitchen?
   a. Passover
   b. Chanukah
   c. Rosh Hashanah

2. And what is the name of the specific ritual feast that marks said holiday?
   a. Iftar
   b. Seder
   c. Torah

3. What is the name the Jewish gang has given to the goat?
   a. Inspector Campbell
   b. Darby Crash
   c. Tommy Shelby

4. Meantime, up in Brummie-land, who has been arrested for fighting?
   a. Arthur
   b. John
   c. Michael

5. What's Tommy's suggestion that he says will save £2 per month on worming powder for the horses?
   a. Vaseline from the pharmacy
   b. Goldfish in the water trough
   c. Magpies in the nearby trees

6. Campbell says that in order to ensure your dog obeys you, you have to show it …(what) once in a while?
   a. Carrot
   b. Stick
   c. Ferret

7. What's happened to the Shelbys' men in Camden town?
   a. Ten have been arrested and the rest are on the run
   b. A hundred lie at the bottom of the Thames
   c. They've all defected to Alfie's gang

8. Esme is allowed to speak. What's her input into the meeting?
   a. That men have been responsible for all this mess already
   b. That she's spoken to Johnny Dogs, and the Lees will send men to help
   c. That if Tommy's not careful he'll be the next one to be arrested

9. She later proposes a drastic solution that Tommy brushes away. What is it?
   a. That Tommy escapes to France, as his gypsy blood wants
   b. That John takes over the family's London dealings
   c. That Polly and Michael are sent to Wales to hide

10. What does the vile Campbell demand Polly does to seal his horrible deal?
   a. Shout
   b. Cry
   c. Fight

11. What explanation does Tommy give to Curly about shovelling shit?
   a. To remind himself of what he, Tommy, could have been, had things turned out differently
   b. To remind Curly that everyone is expendable
   c. To show the world that he, Tommy, will do anything to keep his family safe

12. Where does Tommy take Grace?
   a. To the dog track
   b. To see Charlie Chaplin
   c. To see Buster Keaton

13. How does Tommy get them to meet?
   a. Tommy knows his bodyguard
   b. Chaplin needs to buy guns
   c. He sneaks in the back door

14. According to Tommy, where was Chaplin born?
   a. In New York's famous Chrysler Building
   b. In Black Patch Gypsy Camp, Birmingham
   c. In Maesgeirchen, North Wales

15. Why is Grace going to Harley Street for treatment?
   a. She has a gunshot wound that just will not heal
   b. She needs some painkillers that are banned in the USA
   c. She is trying to conceive and has been told it's her fault

16. Arthur's turn to wish for what could have been. What does he say he used to be good at?
  a. Drawing pictures of stallions
  b. Singing folk tunes in the pub
  c. Putting engines together on boats

17. In what position does May say that Grace's Secret will come in the race?
  a. Guaranteed top three, no danger
  b. Last of them all unless something's done
  c. Fifth or sixth

18. What has happened to Field Marshall Russell's house?
  a. It's been burnt down by an incendiary device through the letterbox
  b. It's been severely damaged by a machine gun
  c. Nothing – but Russell isn't living there anymore

19. What does that mean for Russell?
  a. He has to find somewhere to live for three months
  b. He must report to Campbell immediately
  c. He has to rebuild his house and needs money

20. As a result, how has Tommy's mission changed?
  a. He must now follow Russell wherever he goes
  b. He will assassinate Russell at the Epsom Derby
  c. He is off the hook and is free to go

SERIES TWO: EPISODE SIX

The end of the series. But is it the end for Tommy? How will he get things straightened out with London? And what's Campbell's latest plot to get rid of Shelby? As for the races, can the family take back control from Sabini? Grace drops a bombshell of her own, making the horse's name both a foreshadow and an irony. Thomas, though, looks like he's going to face a lonely death in the mud, just like the numerous soldiers of the Great War. This episode turns it all up to 11, so strap in.

1. To whom is Tommy writing his potentially incendiary letter?

    a. The King of England
    b. Winston Churchill
    c. The *New York Times*

2. And who specifically is the letter addressed to?
   a. Mr Charles Ransom Miller, Editor
   b. His Grace Winston Tiberius Churchill, BSE
   c. The Glorious King Albertini III

3. Which unlikely character has Tommy roped in to his orbit to assist him?
   a. Ada
   b. James
   c. Daniel

4. How is Arthur getting out of prison?
   a. All ten witnesses withdrew their statements at 9pm
   b. Campbell busts him out with an explosion
   c. It was a case of mistaken identity

5. Tommy has presented Alfie with a document saying that Solomons will get 20 per cent of the Shelbys' business. Alfie responds with a document of his own, which has a different percentage. What is it?
   a. 50 per cent
   b. 100 per cent
   c. 35 per cent and a ratchet back once he makes his investment back

6. What did Tommy stop to do?
    a. Tie a shoelace
    b. Kill a cockroach
    c. Comb his hair

7. And what did he say he did when doing so?
    a. Wired up a hand grenade to a rum barrel
    b. Left a bundle of used notes near the barrels
    c. Changed his shoes to ones with razors in

8. How long in jail would one get for being arrested on a racetrack in possession of a loaded weapon?
    a. A month
    b. A year
    c. Twenty years

9. At what time will there be, according to Tommy, an 'incident' in the owners' enclosure?
    a. 2.30pm
    b. 3pm
    c. 4.15pm

10. As a result, who will all the police be looking for?
    a. Tommy
    b. Campbell
    c. Polly

11. What's Grace's pre-race revelation?
   a. She's left her New York husband
   b. She's going back to the Secret Service
   c. She's pregnant and it's Tommy's

12. What's Lizzie's job?
   a. To take a certain soldier to a quiet place at 3pm
   b. To run on to the track and delay the race
   c. To look after Arthur while the race is on

13. Tommy tells Campbell that he knows what the latter did to Polly, and what happened to Michael in jail. What's his aphorism about today and tomorrow?
   a. Today, either Tommy or Campbell will be dead, and wake up tomorrow in hell
   b. Today, either Campbell or Grace will be dead, and nobody will mourn either
   c. Today, someone will win the race, but tomorrow they'll wake up skint

14. How does Russell meet his maker after several missteps in the plan?
   a. Tommy manages to shoot him with Russell's own gun
   b. Lizzie shoots him in the back of the head
   c. Tommy and Lizzie throw him off the balcony together

15. How does Tommy throw the officers off the scent?
    a. He says Lizzie did it and ran away
    b. He says he heard Irish voices and a gunshot
    c. He says Russell has shot himself after losing the race

16. What do the Blinders burn once the police are all distracted?
    a. The paddock, in which the horse trainers are sleeping
    b. The gambling/racetrack licences of the Sabinis' bookies
    c. The entire roster of horse owners, so they can steal horses

17. Why, according to Tommy, was Alfie upset with the Sabinis again?
    a. They started telling everyone that the Jewish gang were finished
    b. The Sabinis started a rival distillery of rum next door to Alfie's gaff
    c. They broke a promise that Alfie's bookies could be at Epsom

18. Drama! Tommy is kidnapped. But by whom?
    a. Nick Cave and the Bad Seeds
    b. The Red Right Hand
    c. The White Hand Fascists

19. Who finally offs Campbell, doing it with a badass sign-off?

    a. John
    b. Esme
    c. Polly

20. Tommy is taken out to a field and there's an open grave waiting for him. He resigns himself to the fate that's been stalking him for years. But what happens, and why? No multiple choice here, let's have it in your own words, please. And the episode still has an intriguing coda to it...

SERIES TWO: SOUNDTRACK

This series is dominated by two acts that indie kids of a certain age will know inside out. Plenty more heroes and offbeat tracks to think about here, too. We're testing your musical knowledge here, whether in the show or not – so dig deep!

1. Which female indie star of the 1990s has several tracks throughout the season?
   a. P.J. Harvey
   b. P.J. Proby
   c. D.J. Fontana

2. And which Aussie dark lord of indie/rock/punk did she famously date in the 1990s?
   a. Nick Lowe
   b. Nick Cave
   c. Plato Cave

3. Guitar-a-rama here and there's a bunch of songs courtesy of a Sheffield bunch of scruffs. What's that band's name?
   a. Deerhoof
   b. Reverend and the Makers
   c. Arctic Monkeys

4. It's not on the soundtrack, but can you name that band's biggest/breakthrough hit?
   a. 'I Bet You Look Good On The Dancefloor'
   b. 'Love Is Like A Rollercoaster'
   c. 'Give Me Just A Little More Time'

5. There's a rockin' duo featured here too – unusually, they have no guitarist. The bass player is the vocalist. Can you name them?
   a. Royal Blood
   b. Thompson Twins
   c. White Stripes

6. Which grizzled country superstar provides the affecting version of 'Danny Boy'?
   a. Waylon Jennings
   b. Johnny Cash
   c. D. Wayne Love

7. That musician famously did a hugely emotional cover of a song by Nine Inch Nails in 2002. Can you remember which track?
   a. 'Head Like A Hole'
   b. 'The Perfect Drug'
   c. 'Hurt'

8. BRMC's track 'River Styx' is heard. What does BRMC stand for?
   a. Break Red Machine Code
   b. Black Rebel Motorcycle Club
   c. Brian Reed's Movie Countdown

9. That band name is taken from a seminal outlaw gang movie. Can you name it?
   a. *The Wild One*
   b. *East of Eden*
   c. *The Wild Ride*

10. Finally, who was the star of that movie?
   a. Jack Nicholson
   b. Marlon Brando
   c. Elvis Presley

PEAKTIONARY

You Will Need: Paper and a pencil; if you've got access to a white board, a blackboard, an office flipchart or an electronic version of any of the above that everyone can see, then all the better, but it's not essential.

How to Play: One person draws a character/location/situation/scene etc. from *Peaky Blinders* and the first to guess it is the winner. They then have to draw a scene, and so on.

Variation One: One person does *all* the drawing and the rest of the people are split into two teams. First to, say, five correct answers wins. You'll get used to shouting things out and therefore the drawer must have final say on who was first!

You might also prepare by writing a whole bunch of characters, scenes, foods, drinks, places, clothing, guns, cars etc. on loads of small strips of paper. Fold these up so nobody can see what's on them, and put them in a hat/saucepan/receptacle. This takes the pressure off the drawer and makes sure all the subjects are legitimate *Peaky Blinders*-related themes.

If you feel inclined, you can appoint an additional person as referee. Their tasks include deciding who shouted out first; passing a random piece of paper to the drawer; arbitrating if the drawing doesn't actually look like the thing on the piece of paper; timekeeping on their phone or stopwatch. If you wish, you can ramp up the pressure by giving a maximum of (e.g.) ten seconds per drawing!
A team may pass if they don't know the answer and go on to the next piece of paper.

Variation Two: Two teams, taking it in turns. Each designates a single drawer, who has, for example, a minute to draw their word/themes one by one. Each team has a minute and the highest score wins.

Variation Three: Two teams, at the same time – as above but the play is concurrent! You'll have to be pretty on the ball as a referee to keep that one in check, folks, but remember that your word is final.

Variation Four: Two teams, either taking it in turns or at the same time, but after the drawer has had their turn and the guess has been successful or unsuccessful the next person in the team steps up to take over the drawing.

Let's not be *that* person, though...
Note that you can't draw multiple things on the same piece of paper/page, and of course you must not speak at all or write any words on your drawings. You must not act out the scene or use any charade-type actions to try and get your team to guess quicker. Don't be a naughty sausage – it's all just in fun.

To put it another way...
Any cheating is frowned upon, by order of the Peaktionary Blinders.

SERIES THREE

SERIES THREE: EPISODE ONE

Any episode that starts with the joyous pageantry of a happy wedding day is only foreshadowing that there's intrigue, trickery and quite possibly misery to come. At the start of Series Three, two more years have passed so it's 1924 and Tommy and Grace are tying the knot. Tommy's secret tasks continue; the Russians enter the field of play; and of course there's a big horserace. Business as usual, then, in the world of the Shelbys – with all the shades of light and dark that brings.

1. Lots of Grace's family are dressed in uniforms – what kind?
   a. Cavalry
   b. Captain
   c. Commander

2. Which ironic hymn do the choirboys sing at the start?
   a. 'Silent Night'
   b. 'In the Bleak Midwinter'
   c. 'Jesus Wants me for a Sunbeam'

3. Tommy tells Polly playfully to inform the Lee girls he's counted the… what?
   a. Chairs
   b. Paintings
   c. Plates

4. Tommy lays down some ground rules for his wedding. No cocaine, no sport, and despite the provocation, no…?
   a. Stealing
   b. Fighting
   c. Eating

5. Where does Polly's new potential suitor say he is a refugee from?
   a. Spain
   b. Germany
   c. Russia

6. With whom does Lizzie's absent new man apparently have connections?
   a. The Naples boys
   b. The Rome lads
   c. The Juventus kids

7. To which three things does Tommy suggest a toast is raised?
   a. Love, family, children
   b. Peaky Blinders, cavalry, the future
   c. Love, peace, marriage

8. Most of Grace's side of the family think her first husband died in an accident. But what does Tommy reveal really happened?
   a. Suicide
   b. Murder
   c. Annulment

9. The Russians operate differently. What is a weakness for them, but a strength for Tommy?
   a. Drinking
   b. Family
   c. Travel

10. According to the Russian guest, what is the codename?
   a. Zhivago
   b. Vodka
   c. Constantine

11. Betting is allowed after all – but this time, where do any proceeds go?
   a. To the Crown for thanks
   b. Shelby Foundation charity
   c. To the Bridesmaids

12. Tommy is told he has powerful enemies. Who specifically is said to watch him closely?
   a. The British Government
   b. The Irish Republican Army
   c. The Soviet Embassy

13. Where does the girl put the money after she snorts a line of coke?
   a. In her cleavage
   b. In her garter belt/stockings
   c. In her purse

14. Who is the go-between, according to Grace, in the Russian weapons deal?
   a. Oswald Mosley
   b. Arthur Shelby
   c. Winston Churchill

15. But why must it all be kept a secret?
   a. The guns are stolen
   b. It's against the law
   c. It's against government policy

16. What does Tommy promise Grace while they dance?
    a. That there will never be guns in the house and their son Charles will never see one
    b. That Churchill will never sit down to eat dinner with Grace
    c. That he will take her to Moscow one day and they will be revered

17. Who was the 'Duchess' told to give the money to?
    a. Mr Kaledin
    b. Mr Candelabra
    c. Dr Schuster

18. Who is paying the Shelbys?
    a. The reds
    b. The greens
    c. The whites

19. What will the Shelbys use the money to buy?
    a. The wharf at Boston docks
    b. The pier at New Jersey
    c. The boardwalk empire

20. Who ends up killing the Russian?
    a. Arthur
    b. Tommy
    c. Michael

SERIES THREE: EPISODE TWO

Trouble is never far away from the Peaky Blinders boys, and this time it's John who sets off a train of events culminating in a serious incident. Michael, meanwhile, is beginning to show his capacity as a mover and shaker in the mould of his mentor Tommy, albeit behind the latter's back. There's the Italian mob to deal with, as well as an apparent man of the Lord with a distinctly devilish mutt in tow…

1. What does Tommy want (aside from fear)?
    a. The keys to bays 4, 5 and 6
    b. The contract for the grain master's job
    c. 20 per cent of all earnings in the second quarter

2. What's in Bay 4?
   a. Completed Type 40s and Type 21s waiting for the paint shop
   b. Spare parts from crashed aeroplanes in the area
   c. Mostly bales of hay and various farming goods

3. And Bay 5?
   a. Nothing in particular
   b. Paint shop and parts
   c. Rum and whisky

4. Bay 6?
   a. Red cloaks and soldiers' uniforms
   b. A consignment of dresses
   c. Old stock in storage

5. What name does Special Branch give to the 'Vigilance Committee'?
   a. Section B
   b. Section C
   c. Section D

6. How many armoured vehicles are there?
   a. 28
   b. 27
   c. 26

7. What train should Tommy catch?
   a. The mail train
   b. The slow train
   c. The milk train

8. What was the name of the restaurant, which was burnt down, and in which street? Two points at stake here.
   a. The Taste of Rome, Farringdon Road
   b. The Little Venice, Forge Street
   c. Sampdoria Deliciosa, Liverpool Street

9. Who, instead of injecting horses with cocaine, took it with his cousins?
   a. Derek Bin
   b. Tommy Lee
   c. Danny Lee

10. Who is Vicente Changretta's son vowing to kill, and why?
   a. John, because he threatened to shoot him in the knees
   b. Tommy, because he wasn't allowed to go to the wedding
   c. Arthur, because he short-changed him on a Tokyo deal

11. John's unrepentant, even in the face of Polly's plan to smooth it all over. But what's her idea?

   a. That Tommy will go to the Changrettas with a peace offering and apologise
   b. That Lizzie will apologise and break up with Vicente's son
   c. That John will be promoted within if he just keeps his mouth shut

12. What was the fate of Mr Romanov's toe?

   a. It got stuck to a steel deck
   b. It swelled up to the size of an apple
   c. A dog ate it after it fell off

13. Hang on, though, where the hell is that accent of Romanov's meant to represent?

   a. Russia? Via Ireland and the Netherlands?
   b. God only knows
   c. Might as well be Mars

14. What's John's solution to the Changretta situation?

   a. He beats up Lizzie's boyfriend Angel and warns him off
   b. He leaves Birmingham and skips the country
   c. He tells Tommy that Arthur's lost his mind

15. Surprisingly, Tommy says John did the right thing. What's his position here?

a. If the Shelbys lift their heel from the Italians' necks, the latter will come after the Blinders
b. If an Italian is backed into a corner, he will fight with the strength of ten men
c. London is nothing if Birmingham is not a secure place for the family

16. What has the Birmingham Charity Commission agreed to ignore, in order to grant Grace and Tommy a licence within the next month?

a. The stench of corruption that pervades capitalism
b. The lack of health and safety provision
c. Three rotten floorboards upstairs in their house

17. What does the Father tell Tommy that the Odd Fellows want him to know?

a. That any deviation from their instructions to Tommy will have consequences
b. That the Italians are not to be trifled with under any circumstances
c. That the Jewish gangs are regrouping so he must take heed

18. If Tommy visits his sister again, what is he told will happen to her?
    a. She will never walk again
    b. She will die crossing the road
    c. She will be shot in the face

19. We finally find out the Father's name. What is it and where is he from?
    a. Father Todd Unctious, from Craggy Island
    b. Father Erson Fing, from the Farrar Road Home
    c. Father John Hughes, from St Mary's Boys Reformatory

20. The Duchess, giggling, tells Tommy something about the sapphire. What is it?
    a. That it's hers and she'll do anything to get it back
    b. That it was cursed by a gypsy
    c. That it's entirely fake and made of Venice Glass

HELEN McCRORY

Polly Shelby, aka Elizabeth Gray – matriarch of the Shelbys and the aunt of Thomas, Arthur, John, Finn and Ada. Kept things ticking over and more while the brothers were fighting in the Great War, and after their return became the one to rule calmly over disagreements; later regained her mystical second sight in the most testing of circumstances. Polly was played by the wonderful Helen McCrory, who sadly left us in 2021, aged just 52. Helen's career achievements are numerous, so let's just remind ourselves of what a wonderful actress she was.

1. Where was Helen born?
   a. Paddington, London
   b. Withington, Manchester
   c. Todmorden, Cumbria

2. At which specialist institution did she study her craft?
    a. RADA
    b. Drama Centre London
    c. Institute of Popular Art

3. In 1990, she made her professional stage debut. Which play was it?
    a. *An Ideal Husband*
    b. *A Woman of No Importance*
    c. *The Importance of Being Ernest*

4. And by which playwright is that piece?
    a. Joe Orton
    b. Oscar Wilde
    c. Harry Wiggins

5. Toughie here, for the real theatre-heads. What's that author's full name?

6. Back to Helen – she played one of the main characters in *Macbeth* at the very special venue of Shakespeare's Globe in Southwark, London. Which character?
    a. Banquo
    b. Lady Macbeth
    c. Thelonius

7. Helen played a wealthy countess in another Shakespeare play, *Twelfth Night*. Name that character!
   a. Olivia
   b. Wilde
   c. Coleman

8. Lastly in our brief Shakey diversion, which character did Helen play in a West End run of *As You Like It*?
   a. Rosalind
   b. Celia
   c. Phebe

9. From the Court of Duke Frederick to the court of Queen Elizabeth II. Helen played this person twice in movies, both in *The Queen* (2006) and *The Special Relationship* (2010). Name the real-life character.
   a. Queen Elizabeth II
   b. Princess Diana
   c. Cherie Blair

10. And what was that character's real-life occupation?
   a. The Queen
   b. Barrister
   c. Landmine clearer

11. *Harry Potter* time. Helen played whom in three movies in the franchise?
   a. Narcissa Malfoy
   b. Rowena Ravenclaw
   c. Rita Skeeter

12. Name those three movies!

13. Which part was she originally lined up for – and why could she not take up that role?
   a. Bellatrix Lestrange – she was pregnant at the time
   b. Nymphadora Tonks – she couldn't spell it properly
   c. Amelia Bones – the part was written out in the edit

14. And who took over that part instead?
   a. Billie Piper
   b. Katie Mills
   c. Helena Bonham Carter

15. In which *James Bond* movie did Helen portray an MP called Clair Dowar?
   a. *A Quantum of Solace*
   b. *Goldeneye*
   c. *Skyfall*

16. During the height of the pandemic, she and husband Damian Lewis raised over £1 million for what cause?

a. To feed NHS workers from high-street restaurants
b. To buy NHS workers key equipment
c. To send NHS workers to Euro Disney

17. In 2020 Helen appeared in which four-part political TV thriller written by David Hare?

a. *House*
b. *Roadkill*
c. *Tradewinds*

18. And which comedy actor turned serious US TV heavyweight also starred in that show?

a. Stephen Fry
b. Peter Ustinov
c. Hugh Laurie

19. Which topical TV news quiz did Helen present as a guest in 2019?

a. *Breaking the News*
b. *Not The Nine O'Clock News*
c. *Have I Got News For You*

20. One of the final performances from Helen before her tragic death was in a 2021-released animated movie about a female German painter. For a point each, name the movie and the painter.

SERIES THREE:
EPISODE THREE

Thomas Shelby is one person before the events that ended the previous episode, and after the murder of Grace he is someone different. Any belief in humanity he possessed before has been truly decimated; it's arguably only his son Charles that keeps him from complete breakdown. But a loose cannon Tommy is something nobody wants, and he heads off to see a gypsy, who he hopes can take the burden off him. The Soviets, the Italians and the Blinders are all bang at it still...

1. What is the suggested name for the new school?
   a. The Grace Shelby Institute
   b. Thomas Shelby's Home for Boys
   c. The Derek Shelby Centre For Kids Who Can't Read Good

2. Where has Tommy been sleeping?
   a. In Arthur's house
   b. Outdoors
   c. In a hotel

3. Arthur and John did what to Angel?
   a. Booted him out of the UK
   b. Cut his throat in hospital and killed him
   c. Gave him the hiding of his life

4. What happened to most of the South Side Italians?
   a. They escaped towards the Black Country
   b. They were blown up in a pub
   c. They ran away to Scotland

5. What day will the head of the Changretta family sail to New York?
   a. Friday
   b. Sunday
   c. Saturday

6. What job did Mrs Changretta have?
   a. Blossom seller
   b. Teacher
   c. Coal exporter

7. To which country have Tommy and Johnny Dogs gone?
   a. Wales
   b. Scotland
   c. France

8. While Tommy's away, who do Arthur and John teach how to shoot?
   a. Ada
   b. Polly
   c. Michael

9. Arthur says a gun in your hand is better than a pen in your hand. He elaborates, and says it's more like having ... what ... in one's hand?
   a. A winning betting slip
   b. A newborn baby
   c. One's cock

10. What does Arthur say needs to happen to all the men on his list, and why?
   a. They need to be sacked as they're Communists
   b. They need to be given pay raises as they're true Blinders
   c. They need special treatment as they're ex-army

11. What main reason does Ruben give Polly for wanting to paint her? We're not talking about his 'sales pitch' here, by the way.
   a. To capture her great deportment and graceful appearance
   b. To seduce her and – should it please God – to sleep with her
   c. To get close to Tommy so he can make friends

12. What does Tommy want from Madame Boswell?
   a. Absolution
   b. Resolution
   c. Revolution

13. Specifically, what does he bring to her, for her to deal with?
   a. The sapphire, so she can take it and its curse from him
   b. The last menu from the dance, to burn it forever
   c. The ashes of Grace, to scatter under an oak tree

14. What are Mr Changretta's last words to his wife?
   a. 'I will write to you'
   b. 'I love you forever'
   c. 'I didn't do anything'

15. At what point does Tommy say he's going to finally let Mr Changretta die?
    a. When they can hear the blackbirds singing
    b. When the horn of the steamer sounds
    c. When the Last Post sounds

16. As it turns out, what happens to Vicente?
    a. John shoots him
    b. Arthur shoots him
    c. Michael shoots him

17. Who is the spy for the Soviet Embassy?
    a. James Monkland
    b. Jack McVitie
    c. Ike Rusty

18. Where is the upcoming vacancy in the Shelby Company?
    a. Boston, America
    b. Boston, Lancashire
    c. Bangor, Wales

19. The city will be paralysed on what date?
    a. 8 June
    b. 14 July
    c. 21 June

20. What does Tommy write on the 'expenses' napkin?
    a. 'Show me your diamonds'
    b. 'I have nothing to do with this'
    c. 'I have secrets'

SERIES THREE:
EPISODE FOUR

Can you trust even a priest in the world of Peaky Blinders*? All indications seem to be that you absolutely cannot, as we find out from a chain of events in another thrilling episode. Tommy wants to go fully legitimate, but in order to do so there's always one last job to be taken care of. But will he even stay alive long enough to make it happen? As usual, he's right in the firing line…*

1. There's another death to be marked at the start of this episode. Who's gone to meet their maker this time?
   a. Arthur Shelby Snr
   b. Mrs Changretta
   c. Alfie Solomons

2. What was the name of the bar said character had been in?
   a. The Globe
   b. Erson Fing
   c. Mickey Free

3. Who goes to confession?
   a. Polly
   b. Ada
   c. Miranda

4. What's the combination to the safe?
   a. 36-24-36
   b. 24-8-22
   c. 26-10-77

5. Who's been sleeping with Tommy?
   a. Alice
   b. Gertrude
   c. Lizzie

6. How much will the armoured cars be sold for?
   a. £150,000
   b. £1 million
   c. £20,000

7. And in what combination will the payment be?
    a. £75,000 in cash, the rest in stock options
    b. Cash, diamonds and sapphires
    c. Cash, rubies and six pubs in Wolverhampton

8. Aside from £25,000 being doled out in total, to Charlie and Isiah, what is Tommy's intent for the proceeds?
    a. To buy the best horses in Europe
    b. To sort out the Jewish gang once and for all
    c. To purchase legal property in America

9. Who says killing the stag will be bad luck?
    a. Curly
    b. Kerzy
    c. Charlie

10. What do the ladies all decide to do?
    a. Go to the Bull Ring
    b. Go to Wales together for a break
    c. Lock all the doors and drink all the whisky

11. Who is waiting for Tommy in the house?
    a. Father John Hughes
    b. Princess Tatiana
    c. Ada Shelby

12. Why does Tommy ask John to put a nail in one of the Bentley's tyres?
    a. Because they're planning on starting a new garage
    b. So Tatiana has to stay the night
    c. To give him something to do and keep him out the way

13. The Duchess is, to put it mildly, a loose cannon. What notorious game is she keen to play?
    a. Russian Roulette
    b. Lego Soldiers
    c. Hook A Duck

14. Where does Tommy reckon the Georgians keep their treasure?
    a. In the stables
    b. In a bank
    c. Under the house

15. Stefan Radischevski is talked about. The Blinders want him to get a job in the Georgians' house. Why?
    a. He's the best sharpshooter in Georgia
    b. He can speak Russian
    c. He's related to Churchill

16. What does Linda say is the plan for her and Arthur?
   a. To stay put in Birmingham and become linchpins of the community
   b. To become a nun and monk and devote the rest of their lives to God
   c. To emigrate to California and run a general store, and to teach

17. What happens when Tommy goes to kill the Father?
   a. He chickens out at the last minute and cannot do it
   b. He is beaten up by two men who are waiting for him
   c. His gun jams because it has been switched for a faulty one

18. Tommy has to apologise or what will happen?
   a. The Section D/Odd Fellows will take his son
   b. He will be sent to London to face the Italians
   c. Father Hughes will not take his confession

19. If the train is blown up, whose family will be sacrificed?
   a. The Romanovs
   b. The Solomons
   c. The Shelbys

20. Broken, battered and in huge amounts of pain at the end of the episode, Tommy's in bad shape. Who is the only person that Tommy says he can 'see'?

a. Grace
b. Romanov
c. His dad

PAUL ANDERSON

Arthur Shelby, Jnr may be senior to Tommy in age, but he's certainly not the top dog when it comes to leadership. Arthur is also played with clear relish and utmost skill by the actor Paul Anderson; it's obvious he's having an absolute ball getting his teeth into this meatiest of parts. The actor has also had a fairly unusual route to the top of his game, with various jobs during his teens and twenties away from the craft. We've put together a series of questions about this enigma wrapped up in a fantastic moustache for you...

1. Paul is from South London, but whereabouts?
   a. Kensington
   b. Kennington
   c. Kensal

2. Let's all get Paul a birthday card! But hang on, we need to know when that is, don't we? What date and year was he born?

   a. 12 February 1978
   b. 24 March 1980
   c. 29 February 1979

3. According to the man himself, he was at a dinner party with his girlfriend, telling stories to the table. A certain famous actor was impressed by Anderson's way with words and asked if he'd ever thought about becoming an actor himself. But who was that?

   a. Ricky Gervais
   b. David Jason
   c. Ralph Fiennes

4. It wasn't until age 25 that he did something about his budding skills, though. Which drama school did he eventually enrol in?

   a. RADA
   b. Paul and Barry's Rotherham School of Dramatic Arts
   c. Webber Douglas Academy of Dramatic Art

5. He had a friend from Fife who wrote pieces in which Paul performed at the Royal Court Theatre. What's the name of that Scottish playwright?

a. Gregory Burke
b. Alan Cummings
c. Gregor Fisher

6. Anderson made a notable appearance in a 2014 British thriller, directed by Yann Demange and written by said playwright and friend. What was the name of that movie?

a. *'82*
b. *'71*
c. *'69*

7. And what was the name of Paul's character in that film?

a. Corporal Jackie Swearinger
b. Sergeant Leslie Lewis
c. Sergeant Mark McGowen

8. He was in a movie about footy hooligans before that, though. Name the 2009 film that revisited a 1989 TV movie by Alan Clarke.

a. *The Boot Boys*
b. *London's Burning*
c. *The Firm*

9. Anderson played lead character Bex, head of the fighting gang of which Premiership football team?
   a. West Ham United
   b. Tottenham Hotspur
   c. Manchester United

10. Staying with movies, in 2015 he appeared in which violent Leonardo DiCaprio Western?
   a. *The Good, The Bad and The Ugly*
   b. *The Revenant*
   c. *The Unforgiven*

11. And what was unusual about the name of his character in that movie (no multiple choice here, folks!)

12. The year 2015 again and another film as Anderson's career hots up. His character Caleb Chappel is part of which nautical drama movie?
   a. *In the Heart of the Sea*
   b. *Under the Boardwalk*
   c. *Jaws V: Radioactive Bastards*

13. Which future *Peaky Blinders* castmate is the second mate in that movie?
   a. Helen McCrory
   b. Cillian Murphy
   c. Sam Neill

14. Another year, another Western. *Brimstone* hit the theatres in 2016. Which antipodean actor starred in this psychological, somewhat mystical piece?

  a. Kylie Minogue
  b. Guy Pearce
  c. Ian Smith

15. Anderson's character, Frank, has a thoroughly disreputable profession. What is it?

  a. Cattle rustler
  b. Gun smuggler
  c. Brothel owner

16. The Aussie actor we just spoke about directed this movie, all about a certain sleuth whose adventures were first written by Sir Arthur Conan Doyle. Paul played a character called Sebastian Moran. What's the name of the movie?

  a. *Sherlock Holmes: A Game of Shadows*
  b. *Philip Marlowe and the Cross-hatch Madness*
  c. *Miss Marple's Chainsaw Frenzy*

17. Which duo played the titular detective and his doctoral sidekick respectively?

  a. Paul Harman and Barry David
  b. Robert Downey Jr and Jude Law
  c. Stephen Fry and Jared Harris

18. Which sport is Anderson regularly associated with?
   a. Football
   b. Tai Chi
   c. Boxing

19. Which two top performers in that sport did he appear in a trailer with?
   a. Tyson Fury and Oleksandr Usyk
   b. Bruce Lee and Chuck Norris
   c. Duncan Ferguson and Roy Keane

20. Which top-of-the-range motorcycle was Paul spotted riding in 2024?
   a. Harley-Davidson
   b. BMW
   c. Rotoscope

SERIES THREE:
EPISODE FIVE

Is Tommy finally in a position from which he can't manoeuvre? He's been physically half-destroyed by Father Hughes' gang and this time it's taking him months to recover. That said, vengeance is always close to hand; and there's alliances to be had with old sometimes-foes. What will become of their dealings with the Georgians? Tommy is playing dangerous games as is his wont, and an unexpected person comes forward to deal with the Priest...

1. Let's start with the matter of the Priest. Who says they want to do the deed?
   a. Arthur
   b. Polly
   c. Michael

2. That person has a specific reason which is only hinted at. Something happened – but when?
   a. When Arthur picked him up from the station
   b. When Polly confessed to him
   c. When Michael was a boy

3. Why did Tommy pour his medicine away? No multiple choice here, just an explanation please.

4. Why won't the guns work?
   a. All their firing pins have been removed
   b. They've rusted up in the damp warehouse
   c. They've lost all the shells that came with them

5. Why won't Johnny and the Lees be moved on from outside of Hampton Court Palace?
   a. It's a special camping place
   b. Tommy has bought the land
   c. They have dispensation from the King

6. How much will the families get for their troubles?
   a. £100
   b. £500
   c. £5,000

7. What ironic name does Alfie Solomons give on arrival at the house?

   a. The Wandering Jew
   b. Alfie the Breadman
   c. Alf a Sixpence

8. Which item does Arthur pick up, barely pushing his absolutely consuming anger down?

   a. A doorstop
   b. An ashtray
   c. A crucifix

9. According to Tatiana, the Cossacks are on guard because…?

   a. It's their nature to be suspicious of outsiders
   b. They do so every time the treasury is opened
   c. They're training for the frontline

10. Why do John and Arthur have to get naked? Another one for an explanation-based answer.

11. What's the name of Michael's girl friend (not necessarily 'girlfriend' at this point)?

   a. Charlene
   b. Charlotte
   c. Charmaigne

12. What's Ada's new job title?
    a. Head of House Purchasing
    b. Head of Agreements and Special Ops
    c. Head of Property and Acquisitions

13. Where's Polly going in the car?
    a. To see the portrait painter
    b. To see the police
    c. Just for a drive to clear her head

14. What does Stefan say the Prince wants from him?
    a. That Stefan performs oral sex on the Prince
    b. That Stefan services the Prince's wife in front of him
    c. That Stefan cleans the house naked

15. Why does Alfie say that he doesn't feel trusted?
    a. He's been kept in a dark room on his own
    b. He's tied up at the wrists
    c. He's been told to go back to London

16. How does Alfie know Russian?
    a. Through his mother
    b. Through his father
    c. Through his cousin

17. What legendary item does Alfie take to complete the deal?

   a. An original Romanov necklace from Crimea
   b. A six-hundred-carat diamond from St Petersburg
   c. An original Fabergé egg

18. To an extremely apt soundtrack of Leonard Cohen, Tommy and Tatiana sleep together. What's the Duchess' special move on this occasion called?

   a. Shaslik, originally a Shahin prayer
   b. Khlysty a Siberian prayer
   c. Khrsty, a Bahnbyry soul

19. There's a meeting of old friends as the Blinders meet up with the Tipton Clay Kickers. But what's a 'clay kicker'?

   a. A special gun runner
   b. Highly trained lookouts
   c. Skilled tunnellers

20. If Michael pulls the trigger as requested, what does Polly say she'll do?

   a. Bring down the whole organisation around Tommy's ears
   b. Go straight to Inspector Moss with all the details
   c. Dig a grave for Tommy and put him in it

SERIES THREE: EPISODE SIX

Distractions, accusations, double-crosses and devilish instructions – that's the vibe of the final episode of a rambunctious third series of Peaky Blinders. *Doubts over an old foe's temporary allegiances surface while a matriarch has second thoughts and the Georgian scheme comes to a head. But will anybody get away Scot-free from their nefarious pasts and presents? It's a denouement to the series that's both unforgettable and shocking in equal measure. What else do we expect by now?*

1. It's called the *Grace Shelby Institute for Orphaned Children*, but how does Polly describe it on the lectern?
    a. The *Grace Shelby Institute for Non-Insured Children of the Poor*
    b. The *Grace Shelby Institute for Peaky Blinders*
    c. The *Grace Shelby Institute for Children and Orphans in Birmingham*

2. What will not happen to the kids who enter the Institute?

  a. They will never be made to feel foolish or uneducated in polite company
  b. They won't be sent to the colonies, separated from kin, or made to work
  c. They will not be made to go to the rich man's wars ever again

3. What colours are there in the crucifixion on the window of Father Hughes' new office?

  a. Black and blue
  b. Orange and red
  c. Green and yellow

4. Tommy fatefully lets go of Charles, but how is that situation engineered?

  a. Tommy is taken to the bar, where he needs both hands to hold a drink and nibbles
  b. Arthur takes Charles off him so he can show the little lad how the car works
  c. The ladies of the War Widows' Institute present him with a horse statue and want a photo

5. But what happens?

  a. The nurse and Charles get into a car
  b. The ladies hit Tommy over the head with the horse
  c. The nurse puts Charles to bed upstairs

6. Who has Charles?
   a. Alfie Solomons
   b. The Oddfellows
   c. The police

7. What must Tommy do in order to get Charles back?
   a. Blow up the train and scatter implicating notes in the wreckage
   b. Pretend to blow up the train and make sure he gets arrested
   c. Nothing further – any more moves and it's curtains

8. What else does Father Hughes reveal that he knows about?
   a. Arthur's plan to leave the UK
   b. The tunnel to the strongroom
   c. The uninsured cars on the fleet

9. What is Tommy's deadline to hand over the jewels?
   a. Midnight
   b. Dawn
   c. Midday

10. Which three items does Tommy tell John and Arthur he needs by midday the next day?
   a. 50 sticks of BSA dynamite, 300 yards of cable and six detonators
   b. A bomb, a pair of gloves and a tin bath
   c. 500 sticks of IRA dynamite, a roll of good cable and a reliable lighter

11. What's on Alfie's list?
   a. All the people in Britain who hate the Soviets
   b. All the people in Britain who want a Fabergé egg
   c. All the people in London who can fence gold

12. Crucially, though, who is *not* on the list?
   a. The richest man in Britain
   b. The richest man in Russia
   c. The richest man in New York

13. Why?
   a. Alfie is sworn never to reveal his name
   b. Alfie has double-crossed Tommy with the Oddfellows
   c. Alfie has brought the wrong list

14. Who stops Tommy doing away with Alfie, and why?
   a. The police, because they don't want to jeopardise the deal
   b. Polly, who says it wasn't Alfie's fault
   c. Michael, who says it will ruin the London truce

15. The locomotive will be blown up if word is not heard by what time?
   a. Midnight
   b. Dawn
   c. Ten o'clock

16. Who runs in – too late – to say Charles is safe so the train need not be blown up?
   a. Michael
   b. Finn
   c. Tommy

17. Who needs to sign a certificate of authorisation?
   a. Tatiana
   b. Tommy
   c. Moss

18. Which specific place on Father Hughes' body does Michael slice?
   a. His chest
   b. His arm
   c. His eye

19. Why does Tommy tell the family that they'll likely never be accepted by what we might call 'high society'?
   a. Because of where the Shelbys came from
   b. Because they've done too much killing
   c. Because there are no places at the table

20. What bombshell does Tommy lay on the family at the end of the episode?
   a. That he's leaving immediately for Nova Scotia
   b. That Polly and the painter are to be married the next day
   c. That the police are all lined up to arrest them very soon

SERIES THREE: SOUNDTRACK

The music in this one is taken from a wide range of artists, with some truly epochal sounds courtesy of some of the biggest names in the business. Some of the songs were so new when this third season came out that they were not even released to a wider audience yet – such is the reach of the Blinders. *Let's see how we get on...*

1. A towering Canadian poet and musician was in his 80s when this incredible track was made. Indeed, it was a pre-release song that was used by the production team. Two points: what was the song, and who was the artist?
    a. Leonard Cohen: 'You Want It Darker'
    b. Johnny Cash: 'Hurt'
    c. Tom Waits: 'Down At Devil Bayou'

2. The series also featured a track from another chameleonic artist's oeuvre, taken from the final LP released in his lifetime. Song and artist, please!
    a. Dean Friedman: 'Well Well Said The Rocking Chair'

b. David Bowie: 'Lazarus'
c. David Gilmour: 'Freebird'

3. What was the name of that LP?
a. *Lazarus*
b. *Blackstar*
c. *Golden Tongue*

4. Staying with that fantastic artist for a mo, what's his real name?
a. Zowie Bowie
b. Derek Dick
c. David Jones

5. You could describe this band as 'final silhouette marionettes' – what is their actual name?
a. The Lovin' Spoonful
b. Kool & The Gang
c. Last Shadow Puppets

6. The Kills have a song included. But how many monkeys are there in the title?
a. 27
b. 28
c. 23

7. 'Burn the Witch' is a song by whom?
   a. Kyuss
   b. Queens of the Stone Age
   c. Josh and the Jumpin' Jacks

8. Complete the name of this Radiohead song which features: 'You And...'
   a. '...Your Shadow'
   b. '...Me, Me And You'
   c. '...Whose Army?'

9. Why should Queen Kwong feel a little bit shameful (name their song)?
   a. 'Baby Did A Bad Bad Thing'
   b. 'I Never Banged Your Window'
   c. 'Baby Got Back'

10. Back on the Simian trail – why, according to Arctic Monkeys, should you not sit down?
   a. '...Cause There's Nowhere To Park Your Butt'
   b. '...Cause I've Moved Your Chair'
   c. '...Cause Standing Desks Are Healthier'

TV EXECUTIVE FOR A DAY

By a wonderful and bizarre set of unrepeatably unlikely circumstances, all of the commissioning editors of all the television channels are suddenly unavailable. Cor, that's unlucky for them, innit? It is, however, extremely fortunate for the rest of us cause we get to play TV Executive for a Day.

How to Play: The basic version involves everybody. Your task is to construct a filled-out pitch for a new television show, but it must be based on either an actor or a character from *Peaky Blinders*. You must think of the following:

* A Snappy Title

* A One-Line Elevator Pitch

* A Cast List

* A Location

* Anything Else

For example, we came up with this:
Title: *Rundle in the Jungle*

Elevator Pitch: Sophie Rundle is airlifted into the Amazon and must survive on her wits for a week.

Cast List: Sophie Rundle, Bear Grylls, and a buncha critters, plus countless possibly poisonous and actually also maybe carnivorous plants.

Location: Amazon River, South America

Extra Info: Bear Grylls is available on the end of a walkie-talkie for advice but can only talk in rhyme for some reason, and Sophie is allowed to swap herself out for either Ant or Dec at any time, but if she does so, they also have to re-record all her parts for all DVD releases of her *Peaky Blinders* appearances.

Variation One: Create a panel of three commiss-ioners, à la *X Factor* and the like. Their job is to sit there in judgement as each other player, one by one, pitches them a different show they've thought of as above. The panel must feed back to the pitcher, and give them a mark out of 10.

The highest-marked pitch wins, and from that exciting moment goes away to make the show at great cost and to brilliant standards. However, by the time it's ready to be broadcast, there's been a change in the upper management and they mothball the show, hiding the tapes away in a locked vault so nobody ever sees the programme. Management have spent all the money hiring Michael McIntyre and flying him out to Goa, where he will present a 24-part series of *Funny Animals Pooing* based on out-takes from already-existing David Attenborough programmes. To everyone's chagrin, it absolutely smashes everything else out of the way and gets viewing figures of 22 million every Saturday night.

Variation Two: The silent pitch. One player has to pitch the show without speaking – so, a version of *Charades* but based on shows that nobody has ever seen before. Can you spread the word about *Rundle in the Jungle* without talking?

SERIES FOUR

SERIES FOUR:
EPISODE ONE

The fourth series begins with most of the Blinders in desperate straits. Of all their problems over the years, it's surely impossible to get out of this one. Well, that wouldn't be a very satisfying narrative road to go down so let's give dubious thanks to Thomas Shelby, who as ever manages somehow to avoid disaster at the very last minute. It's taken its toll on the family, though: their legendary close-knit bond is looser and unlikelier than ever. There's also the son of an old foe out for revenge. Welcome back, folks...

1. What process is supposed to start in January?
   a. New horseracing rules
   b. The appeal
   c. Restructuring

2. What's the name of the King?
   a. Harry
   b. Arthur
   c. George

3. Who was supposed to intervene at the appeal?
   a. The Lord Chamberlain
   b. The Lord Chambermaid
   c. The Queen's Equerry

4. As well as burning the letters, what else has Tommy cheekily and typically asked for?
   a. An OBE
   b. Stables
   c. A passport

5. It's a year later – but at which specific date do we pick up the story?
   a. 23 December 1925
   b. 24 December 1930
   c. 24 December 1920

6. Which new item do we see Tommy wearing?
   a. Red socks
   b. Glasses
   c. Earrings

7. What time is he due at the Singer factory?
   a. 9am
   b. 8am
   c. 7am

8. Who's hosting the big New Year party?
   a. Arthur
   b. Michael
   c. John

9. What's on Tommy's list of three things as he ponders which he should give up?
   a. Sex, freedom, whisky sours
   b. Guns, cocaine, prostitutes
   c. Cake, chips, horses

10. What's the name of the union conveyor causing Tommy a headache?
   a. Jessie Ware
   b. Jessie Eden
   c. Jessie Blake

11. What's Polly running from the house?
   a. Seances
   b. Gambling
   c. Knitting

12. What's Tommy's 'solution' to the pay disparity?
    a. To cut everyone's pay to the same level
    b. To cut the male cutters' pay by five shillings, and raise the females' pay by the same
    c. To raise everyone's pay to the same level

13. With Frances also at the table, how many people will there be?
    a. 26
    b. 27
    c. 28

14. What's on the cards that John, Arthur, etc. receive?
    a. A black hand
    b. A red right hand
    c. A green hand

15. According to Moss, for whom is Luca Changretta a soldier?
    a. The Pinata family
    b. The Spinetta family
    c. The Marinetta family

16. Where will the family meeting be, and when?
    a. Charlie's yard on Boxing Day
    b. John's house on New Year's Eve
    c. Tommy's stables on Christmas Day

17. How much cash does Tommy give to Antonio?
    a. £10
    b. £5
    c. £100

18. Where did chef work before coming to Tommy's employ?
    a. Gordon's, Jamie's, San Marino
    b. Bertorelli, Claridge's, San Marco's
    c. Bangorelli, Cofiegg, Stan Omara

19. What does Tommy give to Johnny Dogs?
    a. A stallion
    b. A mare
    c. A car

20. They're not the Peaky Blinders unless… what?
    a. They're horseracing
    b. They're together
    c. They're winning

SERIES FOUR:
EPISODE TWO

Back in Small Heath, where arguably their hearts never left, the Peaky Blinders are also returned to the heart of matters. Tommy as usual is all about making alliances, but this time has he over-reached? Polly seems determined to get away, and Ada's firmly in the firing line. There's a new kind of business opportunity that could prove irresistible, though everything rests on whether a certain mysterious businessman apparently from Paris can achieve satisfactory results for his own bosses...

1. Polly doesn't want kids in the hospital. Who does she want?
    a. Men who've served
    b. Men who've killed
    c. Family only

2. Where does Esme say she'll take the kids?
    a. To New York
    b. On the road
    c. To Australia

3. From where are the assassins sent to kill the Shelbys?
    a. New Brighton and Birmingham
    b. New York and Birmingham
    c. New Jersey and Seattle

4. Who has Tommy sent a message to?
    a. Aberama Gold
    b. David Gold
    c. Johnny Dogs

5. Why can't the police assist?
    a. They're all out in Wolverhampton
    b. They're expecting strikes and riots
    c. They won't deal with Tommy anymore

6. Two people get shot at the funeral. Who?
    a. Innocent bystanders
    b. Would-be assassins
    c. The Lee brothers

7. Rather than go to the country, where does Linda go?
   a. 57 Watery Lane
   b. 22 Acacia Avenue
   c. 72 Dorrit Street

8. How many bullets did Michael take?
   a. Six
   b. Two
   c. Four

9. Where does Polly want herself and Michael to go?
   a. New York
   b. Scotland
   c. Australia

10. On which date will the boat leave?
   a. 14 February
   b. 26 May
   c. 13 February

11. Aberama wants Charlie's yard. What deal does Tommy offer?
   a. Spin a coin: if it's heads, Aberama gets the yard. Tails, and Tommy has sex with his daughter
   b. Spin a coin: if it's heads, Aberama gets the yard. Tails, and Tommy gets the yard
   c. A straight-out bare-knuckle fight. Six rounds, no quarter given

12. Moss reveals something worrying to Polly. What is it?
   a. That he's to retire within the year, and all deals will be off
   b. That Ada is top of a list of suspected Communists
   c. That Tommy is being investigated for fraud

13. How many of the Shelby Company's factories are in a safe area?
   a. 70 per cent
   b. 50 per cent
   c. None

14. What hunch does Polly have about Aberama Gold?
   a. That he's not really who he says he is
   b. That he's working with Moss
   c. That he wants something other than cash

15. Lo and behold, – another character comes back to join the party. Who is it?
   a. May
   b. Grace
   c. Lizzie

16. Who will be fighting Bonnie Gold?
   a. Curly Kerz
   b. Wayne Francis
   c. Billy Mills

17. At what time is the revolution scheduled?
    a. Noon
    b. 4pm
    c. Midnight

18. What does Bonnie say he could fight, and knock out?
    a. A tree
    b. A horse
    c. A cow

19. Why hasn't Luca already killed Tommy?
    a. He couldn't get close enough
    b. He's saving him until last
    c. He doesn't believe Tommy's guilty

20. What does Luca suggest to Tommy?
    a. That they fight the vendetta with honour
    b. That they have it out right here, right now, right on the polished table
    c. That Tommy buys the vendetta out for £100,000

ANNABELLE WALLIS

Barmaid, undercover agent, lover of Thomas... Grace Burgess is one hell of a character. It took a superb actress to deliver the range of emotional depth, hidden agenda and sheer charisma. Fortunately for any fan of the show, the fabulous Annabelle Wallis was perfect for the part. As you can imagine from someone so talented, Wallis has a wonderful career outside of Blinders, *which we're going to have a good look at right now. How will you get on?*

1. What's Annabelle's middle name?
   a. Sian
   b. Frances
   c. Darlene

2. In which decade was she born?
   a. 1970s
   b. 1980s
   c. 1990s

3. And which English town, situated in Oxfordshire, is she from?
   a. Oxford
   b. Banbury
   c. Henley-on-Thames

4. Annabelle comes from a wider family of acting stock. Her great-uncle on her mother's side was from Limerick, Ireland, and played a significant role in the first two *Harry Potter* movies. But what's his name?
   a. Robbie Coltraine
   b. Richard Griffiths
   c. Richard Harris

5. After that actor's sad death in 2002, who replaced him for the rest of the *Harry Potter* movies?
   a. Christopher Lee
   b. Ian McKellen
   c. Michael Gambon

6. Did you know that Annabelle was raised in Portugal? As a result, she is fluent in four languages. English and Portuguese are obviously two, but what are the others?
   a. Italian and German
   b. Arabic and Farsi
   c. French and Spanish

7. Her first movie break was also an international one. She was in a movie called *Dil Jo Bhi Kahey...* which translates as *Whatever the Heart Says*. But which country did the 2005 piece come from?

   a. Scotland
   b. India
   c. Romania

8. Annabelle really hit the highs when she became a major character in a 2009 Showtime series. It was an historical royal drama. What was it called?

   a. *The Stuarts*
   b. *The Tudors*
   c. *The Joneses*

9. And which queen did she play?

   a. Jane Seymour
   b. Anne Boleyn
   c. Anne of Cleves

10. In 2016, the multi-talented performer provided background vocals on a song called 'Up&Up', alongside Merry Clayton and Beyoncé. It's a song by which British band?

   a. Kaiser Chiefs
   b. Coldplay
   c. Neil Midgeley and the Referees

11. For a time, Annabelle was part of a couple with the singer of said band. What's that vocalist called?
   a. Christopher Cross
   b. Chris Martin
   c. Ian Fraser Kilmister

12. In which 2014 horror film did Annabelle play the character Mia Form?
   a. *Creation*
   b. *Annabelle*
   c. *Ward*

13. Two years later, her character Lina Smit was in which movie created by Sacha Baron Cohen?
   a. *Ali G: In Da House*
   b. *Borat II*
   c. *Grimsby*

14. Annabelle played alongside Tom Cruise in this ancient Egypt fantasy/action-adventure movie, in 2017. Name the film.
   a. *Mission Improbable*
   b. *Scientidiocy*
   c. *The Mummy*

15. This TV drama looked at a certain iconic aeroplane company. Among the stewardesses were Margot Robbie and Christina Ricci. Annabelle was an English stewardess called Bridget Pierce. The show has all sorts of other shenanigans involving the CIA too – ooh, it's fun! What's the series called?

a. *BOA*
b. *DOA*
c. *Pan Am*

16. Annabelle won Best Villain in 2002's *BloodGuts UK Horror Awards* – but for which movie?

a. *Malignant*
b. *Moider Most Horrid*
c. *Madheads on Fire*

17. Every actor eventually has a Christmas movie in their filmography and Wallis is no exception. Hers is described as 'an apocalyptic black comedy'. That's the Chrimbo spirit right there! But what's it called? Other acting talent in this 2021 movie includes Keira Knightley, Matthew Goode and Lily-Rose Depp, if that helps.

a. *God Kill Ye Smelly Gentlemen*
b. *Silent Night*
c. *Deck the Halls*

18. This 2024 Italian thriller is a remake of *7th Floor*, which was released in 2013. It's about a couple going through a divorce but all kinds of gnarly stuff comes out. Can you name it?
   a. *Vanishing Point*
   b. *Extremely Bad Divorce Movie*
   c. *Vanished Into the Night*

19. What's the name of Annabelle's good friend, a fashion designer, with whom she worked in 2020 to raise funds for Age UK?
   a. Georgia Hardinge
   b. Stella McCartney
   c. Georgeat Asda

20. She's a patron of many good causes. This 2018 *Letters Live* event raised funds for Women for Women International, and Annabelle read out a letter by a very famous suffragette. Who?
   a. Christabel Pankhurst
   b. Sylvia Pankhurst
   c. Emmeline Pankhurst

SERIES FOUR: EPISODE THREE

Family and tradition are both themes which loom large as the action is fully under way; Michael continues his long convalescence; Arthur is not where he should be, leading to fatal consequences and internecine problems; we find out more about the pre-war Tommy, who sounds like an actual sweetheart; union and Communist issues continue to muddy the waters; Polly is back in the Shelby bosom but also has plans to go behind Tommy's back. Physically unlikely, metaphorically an absolute narrative bombshell. Oof, there's some shenanigans in Small Heath…

1. Who visits Michael at the start of the episode?
    a. Arthur Shelby
    b. Inspector Moss
    c. Rosemary Johnson

2. They give him a message. What is it?
   a. That he's needed pronto by the Blinders
   b. That he needs to keep his head down for a bit
   c. That his foster father has died in his sleep

3. Where do the new workers mostly come from?
   a. Farmhands from around Worcester
   b. Factory workers from Wolverhampton
   c. Barmen from Barmouth

4. Linda is wearing a new garment that she's keen for Arthur to feel. What material is it and where is it from?
   a. Cotton, from India
   b. Silk, from Japan
   c. Nylon, from New York

5. How did the Shelbys get hold of the photos of Luca Changretta? Explain in your own words please – no multiple choice.

6. What's the plan with the photos?
   a. To circulate them in pubs and street corners, and offer a reward for info
   b. To give them straight to the police, whose new orders are to find the Changrettas
   c. To keep them within the family, so everyone knows their enemy

7. Specifically, who will a copy of Luca be shown to?
   a. Aberama Gold
   b. Tommy Shelby
   c. Michael Shelby

8. Why is this controversial?
   a. According to tradition it's the oldest son, Arthur, who should kill Luca
   b. According to tradition, it's the most successful son, Tommy, who should do it
   c. Aberama Gold is likely to be working with Luca already

9. Arthur was distracted by Linda, but as a result what does he do?
   a. Gets away from Birmingham until the fuss dies down
   b. Kills two of the would-be hitmen
   c. Enlists another hundred men

10. Why shouldn't the men have been able to get into the factory?
   a. The back door should have been locked
   b. It was Sunday and everyone should be in church
   c. There should have been a security guard nearby

11. Why are the Devlin family unsafe in Glasgow?
    a. They are now on the hitlist of the Black Hand
    b. The Blinders have links with Catholic gangs there
    c. The Blinders have sent a team up there already

12. What's the name of Tommy's lost pre-war love?
    a. Greta Jurossi
    b. Kitty Jurossi
    c. Jackie Grioso

13. What happened to her?
    a. She died in an explosion
    b. She died of consumption
    c. She emigrated to New Zealand

14. What did Kitty say Tommy did, when he saw a man beating his horse?
    a. Tommy beat him with his own whip
    b. Tommy shot him in the kneecaps
    c. Tommy hid his shoes for an entire year

15. What potentially devastating info did Kitty also impart?
    a. That Greta was still alive in Camberwell
    b. That Tommy once joined the Communists
    c. That Tommy tried to get away from the war

16. What does Jessie give to Tommy?
    a. A photo of Kitty and Greta as kids
    b. A photo of John and Greta together
    c. A photo of Tommy and Greta together

17. What does Jessie do to the photo Tommy shows her?
    a. Throws it away
    b. Burns it
    c. Nothing

18. Where does Tommy take Lizzie, that he hasn't been since the war?
    a. To the canal
    b. To the pub
    c. To Wolverhampton

19. What does Luca reveal that his mother told him?
    a. That John and Arthur spared her life – and she's given him loads of info too
    b. That Polly is the weak link – and to get to her at all costs
    c. That he should never cross the Peaky Blinders

20. Smooth criminal that he is, what else does Luca say?
    a. That Polly loves a man in uniform
    b. That Polly loves her champagne
    c. That Polly loves to dance

SERIES FOUR:
EPISODE FOUR

Sneakiness pervades the very screen as it seems Polly's under-the-radar deal is paying dividends. A new horse is given an appropriate name by someone who could be described accurately by that moniker. Tommy's spirits export plans are considered. Finn continues his slow initiation into manhood, while Ada gets close to someone that may do harm to the Peaky Blinders. An old mate nips up the road to say hi and helps Tommy out with some very interesting information – but is he already earmarked for his final journey?

1. Who is invited to the 21st birthday commemoration for the deceased Edward?
   a. Tommy
   b. Arthur
   c. Finn

2. But what has Tommy deduced?
    a. That it's a trap
    b. That Arthur's abroad
    c. That Edward is alive

3. What will Johnny and Isiah be selling?
    a. Stolen beef
    b. Stolen lamb
    c. Stolen pork

4. What does Luca tell Michael?
    a. That the deal with Polly is on
    b. That he should join the Mafia
    c. That he's a dead man walking

5. Who gets shot that possibly shouldn't have been?
    a. Tommy
    b. Polly
    c. A policeman

6. What's the name of the new horse?
    a. Dangerous
    b. Disastrous
    c. Delicious

7. Why does May say it's called that?
   a. Because everything around the Shelbys is like that
   b. A horse of that same name once won the Epsom Derby
   c. The horse is prone to kicking and biting other horses

8. Why does May think Tommy might have changed?
   a. It's been two long years and nobody's the same
   b. He's got a nice big house and lots of money
   c. He's lost his wife and his brother

9. Which item of clothing does Lizzie point out on Tommy?
   a. Hat
   b. Shoes
   c. Shirt

10. For how much is the cheque that constitutes May's donation?
   a. £100
   b. It's blank
   c. £200

11. Whose recipe is the gin?
   a. Polly's
   b. Tommy's mother's
   c. Tommy's father's

12. What's the phone number of the betting shop?
    a. Small Heath 442
    b. Small Heath 552
    c. Small Heath 662

13. What news for Lizzie does Polly see in the tea leaves?
    a. That she's going to die
    b. That she's pregnant
    c. That she's a Shelby

14. And what day does Polly say for Tommy to keep free?
    a. Wednesday
    b. Thursday
    c. Friday

15. Which actual date will it be? Polly puts an ominous black star on it...
    a. Friday 1 June
    b. Friday 9 March
    c. Friday 5 February

16. In what division/weight and area is Bonnie Gold registered?
    a. Heavyweight, North West
    b. Lightweight, Wales and Borders
    c. Welterweight, Midlands

17. How much gin will the new operation provide when up and running?
   a. Six gallons a week
   b. 100 gallons a week
   c. 200 gallons a week

18. Shelby Company Limited will give men and women wage parity, in exchange for… what?
   a. An extra hour's work per day
   b. That Jessie sits down and talks to Tommy
   c. That Jessie leaves the area immediately

19. What's Tommy getting, to make sure his starlings problem disappears?
   a. A wolf
   b. A kestrel
   c. An eagle

20. What relation does Alfie say he is to the Southern Counties welterweight champion?
   a. Father
   b. Brother
   c. Uncle

JOE COLE

John Boy Shelby, one of the original brothers, is part of the close-knit early Peaky Blinders. A potent fella, he is the father of seven kids in the show. Johnny may not have made it through the entirety of the Shelby clan's adventurous rise, but without him it may not have happened at all. John is played by British actor Joe Cole, a fresh-faced but experienced player whose career continues to develop. Time to spend a little time with Joe and to fill in some of the biographical and filmological gaps...

1. He's obviously not the same Joe Cole who played football – but what nationality was that 'soccerist' namesake?
    a. German
    b. Scottish
    c. English

2. Joe's brother was also in *Peaky Blinders*. What's his name?
   a. Brian
   b. Finn
   c. Dougal

3. He was born on 28 November 1988. What star sign does that make him?
   a. Scorpio
   b. Sagittarius
   c. Capricorn

4. How is that sign generally represented pictorially?
   a. Twins
   b. A crab
   c. A bowsman

5. What's Joe's middle name?
   a. Trouble
   b. Francis
   c. Michael

6. Which cop show did he make his TV debut in, in 2010?
   a. *The Bill*
   b. *Rozzers FC*
   c. *The Filth*

7. And which TV hospital show did he also appear in, during the same year?

a. *Holby City*
b. *House*
c. *General Hospital*

8. Joe was nominated for a Bafta in an episode called 'Hang the DJ' of which dark futuristic series?

a. *Inside No. 9*
b. *Black Mirror*
c. *Magpie*

9. He played Sean Wallace in which long-running TV street thriller based on a video game?

a. *Gangs of the EPL*
b. *Tomb Raider*
c. *Gangs of London*

10. And in which 2022 mini-series did he play a character made famous in movies by Michael Caine?

a. *The Ipcress File*
b. *Alfie*
c. *The Magus*

SERIES FOUR:
EPISODE FIVE

Ah, Tommy Shelby. Always two steps ahead, as he shows when he quite easily gets out of what looked like the perfect trap. He couldn't have done it without a key collaborator, though: someone with whom he's butted heads quite a few times but also with whom he ultimately is absolutely entwined (and vice versa). Lizzie reveals her situation. Alfie and Luca have an intriguing discussion about the future, and Tommy eventually reveals just why he's cosying up to the establishment…

1. What weapon does Tommy use to fight back against the Italians?
   a. A machine gun
   b. A grenade
   c. A rocket launcher

2. What does Luca propose?
   a. A duel
   b. Peace
   c. Exchange

3. Who stops the contretemps?
   a. Arthur
   b. Polly
   c. Police

4. How did Tommy know the Italians were coming?
   a. Polly received a letter from Luca saying Michael would be spared if she gave him Tommy
   b. Tommy has a spy close to the Mafia, who tells him everything that is happening
   c. Tommy found paperwork pertaining to the Italians among Alfie's luggage

5. What comforting words does the messy Arthur need to hear from Linda?
   a. That nobody can ever get near to him as long as they have each other
   b. That they'll be both in their garden before it's time to plant anything
   c. That he's the head of the family and always has been

6. Which unusual meat does Aberama ask Michael, jokingly, if he's ever had?

   a. Hedgehog
   b. Badger
   c. Mushroom

7. What's the name of Michael's grandmother, according to Polly?

   a. A gypsy princess called Belinda Palmer
   b. A gypsy princess called Birdy Boswell
   c. A gypsy princess called Delilah Osman

8. Polly asks Aberama if he knows a longer way back. He says he knows ways back that would take how long?

   a. A year
   b. A month
   c. Forever

9. Which sex of hare tastes better, according to Polly?

   a. There's no difference
   b. Jill
   c. Buck

10. When did Polly's gift of second sight come back?

   a. When she was pregnant
   b. In the noose
   c. After John died

11. Why does Alfie say he spends half an hour each day with his eyes closed?
   a. To better understand the blind
   b. To seek wisdom in the void
   c. To make the sun shine brighter

12. How many barrels per month does Alfie want to export through New York?
   a. 100
   b. None
   c. 200

13. What else does Alfie think the Italians want from him?
   a. To take their goods over from Italy
   b. To kill Tommy for them
   c. To stop making rum

14. Luca wants his men close to Tommy. How?
   a. In the upcoming boxing match, they will be in the ring as seconds
   b. In the upcoming horserace, they will be in the winners' enclosure
   c. In the upcoming General Strike, they will be with the police

15. What drastic body modification will also need to happen?

    a. They'll all have to get tattoos
    b. They'll all have a finger removed
    c. They'll all be circumcised

16. The ever-entertaining Alfie waits until the last minute to reveal he can do what?

    a. Shoot an apple from 100 yards
    b. Speak Italian
    c. Dance the tango

17. Who is strip-searched?

    a. May
    b. Esme
    c. Ada

18. Who has been 'given' Birmingham?

    a. Colonel Ben Younger
    b. Admiral Ben Older
    c. Captain Asa Hartford

19. What's the total value of the military contract that Tommy has been offered?

    a. £1 million
    b. £2 million
    c. £6 million

20. Bonnie will get a 20 per cent cut if he puts Goliath down in which round?

a. First
b. Tenth
c. Fourth

SERIES FOUR:
EPISODE SIX

Goliath? That's a name which brings back some resonant context, isn't it? The mighty one. That said, in the Bible didn't he… lose? Well, we'll find out what happens when that bell rings with the dangerous Bonnie Gold ready to topple Alfie's big hope from down South. Something shocking happens to Arthur, but beware of Italians bearing white flags. Michael's sent off to the New World, but Tommy as ever has his eyes set on infiltrating the establishment in a typically unexpected manner…

1. To where does Alfie tell Tommy he is moving?
   a. America
   b. Margate
   c. Manchester

2. According to Polly, is Lizzie and Tommy's kid a boy or a girl?
   a. Boy
   b. Girl

3. And what is the kid's destiny, reckons Pol?
   a. To be head of the Shelbys
   b. To be the greatest mother ever
   c. To star in a Hollywood movie

4. Arthur's spotted something awry with the men in Goliath's corner. Which two things do they not 'do' right?
   a. Stand and move
   b. Shout and sit
   c. Towel and water

5. To what, though, does Tommy attribute Arthur's reservations?
   a. The pills
   b. The snow
   c. The atmosphere

6. Arthur follows one of those men – but what happens?
   a. The man was simply going to the toilet, and it's embarrassing
   b. Arthur loses him in the crowd, and goes to sit back down
   c. Arthur gets garrotted seemingly to death, and Tommy shoots his assailant

7. What does Finn do to the other attacker, as told by Tommy?
   a. Take his eyes
   b. Shoot his knees
   c. Break his spine

8. Where is Michael being sent to?
   a. Australia
   b. Reigate
   c. New York

9. Who arrives at Arthur's funeral, waving a white flag?
   a. Luca Changretta
   b. Mrs Changretta
   c. Inspector Moss

10. As a condition of the end of the vendetta, what do the Shelbys need to do?
    a. Sign over all their businesses to the Changrettas
    b. Leave Birmingham entirely forever
    c. Work in the Changrettas' munitions factory

11. Why did Luca let all the Shelbys live?
    a. His mother told him it'd be better, cause then they'd suffer as he took everything
    b. He wanted to show them how dangerous it was working against the Mafia
    c. He tired of all the killing and wanted to go legitimate in business

12. What does Luca demand Tommy does?
    a. Shows him where the door is
    b. Gets on his knees to sign the documents
    c. Redrafts the documents immediately

13. What's the name of the Chicago businessman that the Shelbys have contacted?
    a. Valentino Rossi
    b. Guiseppe Terrromoto
    c. Alphonse Capone

14. Who specifically does Luca single out when he realises his men are working for the Shelbys?

a. Matteo
b. Galileo
c. Guiseppe

15. Tommy and Luca fight. Who enters the fray to bring the final justice?

a. Michael
b. Arthur
c. Polly

16. Arthur sends the goons off with the instruction to tell their boss… what?

a. Not to bother with Birmingham anymore
b. Not to fuck with the Peaky Blinders
c. Never to mention Luca's name again

17. Arthur reveals that Tommy offered him the chance to get away and make a new life. But he's staying. He does, however, have a proposal. What is it?

a. That Tommy takes time off
b. That Polly becomes head of the family
c. That Michael stays in Birmingham

18. What's the name of Alfie's dog?
    a. Sybil
    b. Curly
    c. Cyril

19. Who shoots first?
    a. Alfie
    b. Tommy
    c. Han

20. At the end of the episode, what crazy twist happens? Obviously, this is a massive spoiler so if you don't want to know, leave the quiz right now!
    a. Tommy gives himself up to the police once and for all
    b. Tommy reveals that Alfie is not really dead
    c. Tommy is returned as the Labour Party MP for Birmingham South

SERIES FOUR: SOUNDTRACK

More inky-black sounds and ferociously brilliant tracks to delight. We're gonna delve a little into the music scene of the early(ish) millennium and test your knowledge of prize winners. Series Four even has a couple of cover versions of a very familiar track. So what better place to start than there?

1. These two male frontmen are very different in style, clothing and sound. They both share an independent spirit for sure. And together they provide one of the covers of 'Red Right Hand' in this season. Name the unlikely duo.
a. Jarvis Cocker and Iggy Pop
b. Frank Carter and Ed Sheeran
c. Larry Love and Biggie Smalls

2. This female indie-folk singer-songwriter also takes on the title song of *Peaky Blinders*. Who is she?
a. Laura Lexx
b. Laura Marling
c. Marlene Lovich

3. What was the name of that musician's debut album? Clue: it was nominated for 2008's Mercury Prize.
   a. *Angels and Airwaves*
   b. *Under the Boardwalk*
   c. *Alas, I Cannot Swim*

4. But who won that year's Mercury?
   a. Elbow: *The Seldom Seen Kid*
   b. Radiohead: *Songs For Miserablists*
   c. Foals: *Foals Sing Musichall*

5. Talking of Foals, complete the name of their track which we hear this season: '... Oil'
   a. 'Castor...'
   b. 'Olive...'
   c. 'Snake...'

6. The Kills' song in this series has a title about the heart of which animal?
   a. Cat
   b. Dog
   c. Chinchilla

7. 'Devil Inside Me' is performed by Frank [Who?] and the Rattlesnakes?
  a. Ifield
  b. Walters
  c. Carter

8. Which seminal punk band did said Frank end up guesting with as frontman for various 2024/5 tours?
  a. The Clash
  b. Sex Pistols
  c. Dead Kennedys

9. There's another absolutely magnificent, and rightly feted, track by Nick Cave and the Bad Seeds during Season Four. Which Cave classic is it?
  a. 'Ken Lee'
  b. 'Stagger Lee'
  c. 'Henry Lee'

10. Another Nick Cave and the Bad Seeds all-time classic appears. Name it!
  a. 'Mercy Seat'
  b. 'Mersey Seat'
  c. 'Murder Ballad'

20 QUESTIONS

Players: Two or more

You Will Need: Nothing!

How to Play: Player One thinks of a character in *Peaky Blinders*. The other player/s have to guess who that is – within 20 guesses. Simple, right? Well, not that simple: the guessing player can only ask questions that have a yes/no answer (that is, closed questions, rather than open ones). So, the guessing player might ask as their first question: Are you a man? Player One then says yes or no. The next question might be something like: Are you over 50 years old? Player One then has to say yes or no. As you can see, each question is whittling away at the possible answers to get more and more specific.

A guess also counts as a question – so, if a guesser tries their luck on question eight with: Are you Thomas Shelby? Player One then says yes or no. If it's a 'no' answer, then the next question is question nine.

Once a successful guess has been made, the player who guessed becomes the person who thinks of a character, and the other players must guess who this new character is within 20 questions.

If nobody has guessed correctly after 20 questions, then Player One (or the person thinking of a character) wins. They then reveal the correct answer. A point for a correct guess, and a point to the thinker if nobody guesses correctly.

Variation One: Low-score wins
We eliminate the possible score of zero here – otherwise nobody would ever venture a guess. A successful guess takes the amount of points consistent with the question number that has been reached. So, in our example above, if the guesser was correct with Thomas Shelby, then they would receive eight points. If nobody guesses then they all receive 20 points and the thinker receives one single point for that round. Each player has only one question before their turn comes around. This means Player Three might ask a key question and know the answer – but they cannot guess until Player Four (final guesser) then Player Two (first guesser) have both also had a turn.

Play the same amount of rounds, or multiples thereof, as there are players, and ensure each player has a turn as thinker by going in order of age, passing responsibility to the left after each round.

Variation Two: Thinker in the seat
The same person stays in the thinker's hotseat for an entire round and players take it in turns to ask their 20 questions before moving on to the next game. So, Player One is the thinker. Player Two has 20 questions as usual. If Player Two does not guess, then Player One receives the maximum of one point and Player Two is penalised 20 points. Player One reveals the character then thinks of another one. Then, Player Three has to guess the new character in their turn, and so on. The thinker stays on until every player has had a turn guessing, then Player Two is in the hotseat, and so on. Lowest total score wins.

Of course, characters are only one possible subject. Try things like slang, clothing, pets, drinks, food, Birmingham landmarks, canals... as long as everyone agrees beforehand!

SERIES FIVE

SERIES FIVE: EPISODE ONE

We're in 1929 and money's on everyone's minds. Yes, the Wall Street Crash mashes up the world for millions and the Shelbys are no exception: there are some things that are too big even for Tommy to work his magic on. Talking of the man himself, he's in the spotlight for an inspiring House of Commons speech. You can't leave your past behind, though, and there's always someone looking to get all in your face with it. Is Tommy finally feeling the strain? Welcome to the fifth series...

1. Who is the letter from?
    a. The Angels of Retribution
    b. The Devils of New Jersey
    c. The Marauding Madheads

2. What's the name of Polly's 'beautiful pilot'?
   a. Paul
   b. Pepper
   c. Peter

3. How does Aberama get the bullet out of Finn?
   a. He smacks Finn on the back with some rosemary
   b. He uses a razor blade from Isiah's cap
   c. He uses a surgical saw from the war

4. What language does Charles speak, to the surprise of most?
   a. Rokker
   b. Italian
   c. Welsh

5. We see Tommy shoot the horse. But what does he do immediately afterwards?
   a. Put the gun to his own head
   b. Dig an enormous grave
   c. Fall to his knees to beg forgiveness

6. Why did Michael hold on rather than listen to Tommy?
   a. His stockbroker said the prices would all rebound
   b. He was already too far deep into his plans
   c. He thought Tommy was only joking

7. Where will Lizzie and Arthur be staying when they go to Birmingham?
   a. The Adelphi
   b. Midland Hotel
   c. The Ritz

8. Tommy has a vision of Grace. She asks him if she's a… what?
   a. Ghost
   b. Genie
   c. Ghoul

9. What's Arthur's position in the company?
   a. Chief operating officer
   b. Board supervisor
   c. Chairman

10. The disaster happened in New York, spread to London, and then to… where?
   a. Japan
   b. Australia
   c. Hong Kong

11. What's Leon's surname?
   a. Greene
   b. Brown
   c. Black

12. How much on the dollar is the Nolan Bank of America offering on deposits?
    a. Ten cents
    b. Five cents
    c. Fifty cents

13. What's the name of the landlord that was going to evict the man at the bar, but instead cut the rent in half?
    a. Fellows
    b. Mann
    c. Ladd

14. What does any man who served in France get for free?
    a. A pint of mild
    b. A brandy chaser
    c. A whisky sour

15. How much was the deal worth that Tommy made, in confidence?
    a. £10,000
    b. £25,000
    c. £50,000

16. Who commissioned the deal? Three points here, but no clues.

17. Why is Tommy being urged not to give Ada a hard time?
    a. She's close to the police
    b. She's pregnant
    c. She's got a great idea

18. In Parliament, Tommy says that the people who lost their fortunes recklessly need to do… what?
    a. Make their own breakfast
    b. Fight their own battles
    c. Shine their own shoes

19. Who did Winston Churchill have dinner with when he was in New York?
    a. Al Capone
    b. Michael Shelby
    c. Charlie Chaplin

20. What's the name of the journalist now working for the *London Times*?
    a. Michael Levitt
    b. Mark Lewis
    c. David Jackson

SERIES FIVE:
EPISODE TWO

With action back in Birmingham, it's also back to the track with a new gang in town looking to muscle in on the ever-lucrative racing business. More ominously for the Blinders, perhaps, is the suggestion that they may be working with one of Tommy's more oleaginous political colleagues. Danger is all around, it seems, and indeed there is a message to Tommy that is anything but subtle. He's under pressure again – he seems to thrive on it – but is even his legendary fortune about to turn for the worse?

1. What does the letter say that Tommy finds on the scarecrow?
   a. 'Look ye not forward, nor backward'
   b. 'Look down on earth and see the seeds you have sown'
   c. 'Beware the Black Hand for the black hand knows ye'

2. What instrument is Charles to practise?
   a. Piano
   b. Cello
   c. Violin

3. And what's the name of his teacher?
   a. Mrs Milligan
   b. Mrs Mangrove
   c. Mrs Meaker

4. What is the name of the person in Belfast who is phoning Tommy?
   a. Captain Swan
   b. Captain Swing
   c. Captain Swain

5. With which organisation do they allege Michael was talking on the SS *Monroe*?
   a. The IRA
   b. The UDA
   c. The UVF

6. What time is Michael's train due to arrive?
   a. 4pm
   b. 11am
   c. 3pm

7. Stacker says they have Levitt's diary and one other item. What?
   a. His notebook
   b. His phone book
   c. His clothes

8. Who performed the marriage ceremony for Michael and Gina?
   a. The ship's captain
   b. Charlie Chaplin
   c. Reverend Schumann

9. Who is the mutual acquaintance Tommy and Oswald have?
   a. May Carleton
   b. Jessie Eden
   c. Cat Manners

10. What answer does Tommy give when asked his thoughts on 'the Irish question'?
   a. That the answer is always fine whisky
   b. That he's never been asked it
   c. That it's a question with no answer

11. What would Tommy's new job title be?
   a. Irish Liaison with Special Access
   b. Junior Parliament Advisor to the King
   c. Junior Minister to the Duchy of Lancaster

12. What has appeared in Tommy's dream, and what does it mean? In your own words, this one.

13. What was Michael's plan if he robbed the Shelby money and moved to California?
   a. To invest in the gold rush
   b. To invest in real estate
   c. To invest in the movies

14. The purser lied to Michael about his friends. What did he say they wanted to discuss?
   a. How to get into the horseracing game
   b. How to get their whisky into the United States
   c. How to pay off the police effectively

15. Rather than County Tyrone, where were they really from?
   a. Glasgow
   b. Edinburgh
   c. Belfast

16. And what gang were they from?
   a. Bad Boys, Incorporated
   b. Billy Boys
   c. Belfast Bangers

17. Who do the Billy Boys kill to send a message to Tommy and the Blinders?
    a. Aberama Gold
    b. Bonnie Gold
    c. Polly Shelby

18. Who does Arthur make a new Peaky Blinder, and for what reason?
    a. Billy Grade, to help them fix football matches
    b. Billy Grade, to help them go into showbusiness
    c. Billy Blue, to raise a new army of soldiers

19. Whose birthday is it?
    a. Ruby
    b. Rachel
    c. Paula

20. Who is the only person in the world that Tommy says he can trust?
    a. Arthur
    b. Johnny
    c. Oswald

SOPHIE RUNDLE

Ada is one of the quieter and yet most capable characters in the series, and one around which much intrigue and plot occurs. It's a tough part for anyone to play, and we're exceedingly fortunate that the hugely talented Sophie Rundle takes it in her stride. Outside of Blinders, *she's got a storied career history with tons more to come. Let's take a dive into Sophie's acting chops and see how much we know about her.*

1. In what year was Sophie born?
   a. 1987
   b. 1978
   c. 1988

2. She was born in High Wycombe. Do you know which English county that town is in?
   a. Buckinghamshire
   b. Kent
   c. Yorkshire

3. Sophie studied acting at a specialist university for the arts. Which one?
   a. Royal Academy of Dramatic Art
   b. Liverpool Institute for Performing Arts
   c. Grantham University Arts and Music

4. She made her movie debut in a 2007 indie. It co-starred the marvellous Warwick Davis. What's the name of that film?
   a. *Time to Go*
   b. *Afterglow*
   c. *Small Town Folk*

5. Davis appeared as which Ewok character in *Return of the Jedi?*
   a. Bails
   b. Wicket
   c. Bat

6. Back to Rundle now: in 2012 she had a role in an ITV series about the travails of which famous passenger ship?
   a. DBS *Lusitania*
   b. HMS *Enterprise*
   c. RMS *Titanic*

7. Which movie based on a Charles Dickens book did she also appear in that year?

   a. *Great Expectations*
   b. *Letters by Boz*
   c. *A Tale of Two Cities*

8. Staying with Dickens, the BBC produced a show about characters created by that writer. Sophie was in the 2015 oddity. What was it called?

   a. *Chuzzlewits*
   b. *Dickensian*
   c. *Charlie's Angles*

9. Moving to Arthurian legends now, Sophie was Sefa in an episode called *Arthur's Bane*. Name the 2012 BBC TV series.

   a. *Sword in the Stone*
   b. *Round Table*
   c. *Merlin*

10. Sadly, this ITV drama series was cancelled before it reached a third series. However, it was well-loved by those who saw the programme, which showed the lives and stories of a group of women codebreakers including Sophie's character Lucy, plus a series of murders. What's the series called?

   a. *Itchycoo Park*
   b. *The Bletchley Circle*
   c. *Enigmatic*

11. Sophie did get the chance to play a detective constable in this two-parter based on a Harry Bingham novel. What was the name of that Sky Living series?
a. *Talking to Nobody*
b. *Everyone's an Expert*
c. *Talking to the Dead*

12. Her character, Fiona Griffiths, had a rare mental disorder that is sometimes called 'Walking Corpse syndrome'. It's named for the surname of the first describer, whose first name was Jules. Can you name that illness?
 a. Skywalker syndrome
 b. Cotard's syndrome
 c. Wakanda Delusion

13. What was the name of Sophie's character in *Happy Valley?*
 a. Kirsten McAskill
 b. Kirstie Parry
 c. Kassie Balloon

14. She played four characters in this 2015 TV thriller, based on a play by J.B. Priestley. What's the name of the play and movie?
 a. *An Inspector Calls*
 b. *Dangerous Corner*
 c. *Time and the Conways*

15. In *Brief Encounters*, the 2016 ITV comedy-drama, Sophie played a fictionalised CEO of a lingerie and sex toy company. On which real-life company was the TV show loosely based?

 a. Marks & Spencer
 b. Ann Summers
 c. Victoria's Secret

16. And on whose memoir was the story based?

 a. Jacqueline Gold
 b. Victoria Beckham
 c. Clarissa Rabbit

17. Changing gear entirely – in both senses – what was the name of the show about the New World, in which Sophie played a woman sailing across the world to ostensibly marry a settler?

 a. *Jonestown*
 b. *Smithland*
 c. *Jamestown*

18. David Avery = Freddie Mercury. Mathew Baynton = Kenny Everett. Sophie Rundle = ?

 a. Claudia Schiffer
 b. Gillian Anderson
 c. Princess Diana

19. And what's the name of the actor on that show to whom she later became engaged?

  a. Matt Stokoe
  b. Bobby Stokes
  c. Matt Finish

20. Toughie to end with: what's the name of the playwright responsible for *3 Winters*, in which Sophie portrayed Lucia Kos at the National Theatre in 2014?

  a. Tena Štivičić
  b. Bojan Krčić
  c. Goran Ivanišavić

SERIES FIVE:
EPISODE THREE

Families have dramas of all kinds, don't they?, and the Shelbys are no exception. There's unrest in the ranks with one, perhaps two, wives extremely unhappy. Will they look for a way out? Is that even possible? Aberama is on tilt, and the Billy Boys are ready for a major scrap. Politics is arguably even more cut-throat than the Blinders' bread-and-butter. Tommy's got problems coming from several directions again, but will Michael turn out to be the conundrum he can't find a way to solve?

1. What did the sisters make the 'half-black' child do?
    a. Wash with a different soap
    b. Wash in a different cubicle
    c. Sleep on the floor

2. What happened to the child who was scared of their temper?
   a. They hanged themselves
   b. They ran away
   c. They told the police

3. What is to become of the children?
   a. They will be cast out on the streets
   b. They will be taken to the Shelbys' own institutions
   c. They will get extra cushions

4. How old is Polly?
   a. 40
   b. 45
   c. 50

5. Tommy tells Michael and Arthur that they've previously met some bad men, but this man is…?
   a. The worst
   b. A nobody
   c. The Devil

6. Tommy has been invited to do what?
   a. To leave politics forever and go back to his Birmingham slum
   b. To be the deputy leader of a new political party
   c. To go to France to negotiate with the Mafia

7. To where do you need to go to discuss divorce from a Shelby?
    a. Wales
    b. Scotland
    c. London

8. What does Lizzie say will happen to the man that Linda is talking about?
    a. That he will be banished to Spain
    b. That he will die with no eyes
    c. That he will be welcomed if he is honest

9. What game are Ben and Karl playing?
    a. Draughts
    b. Backgammon
    c. Chess

10. Who does Aberama say will look after him?
    a. God
    b. His brother
    c. His sister

11. Which family does he say he needs to find?
    a. The Furys
    b. The Tornados
    c. The Blakes

12. Where does Michael suggest Tommy goes to see a doctor?
    a. Margate
    b. Glasgow
    c. London

13. What's the name of Ben Younger's superior?
    a. Colonel Christopher Robin
    b. Colonel Patrick Wyatt
    c. Colonel Andrew Jackson

14. What does Gina plan to do?
    a. Go to New York with Michael and the baby
    b. Go to California with Michael and the baby
    c. Stay in Birmingham and join the family

15. What are Lizzie's stipulations to Tommy?
    a. That he does not have sex with others in their house, or within a day of holding the kid by the hand
    b. That he goes to London immediately and annuls Arthur's marriage before it goes any further
    c. That he doubles her pay and that he vows never to shoot another horse

16. There's good in Arthur's heart, he says, but as for his hands...?

   a. He can't tell anyone what they do
   b. They belong to the Devil
   c. They do only Shelby work

17. How many grenades does Arthur ask Curly for?

   a. One
   b. Two
   c. Three

18. Who does Arthur tell the Billy Boys to take a message to?

   a. Phil McCracken
   b. Jackie McGuinness
   c. Jimmy McCavern

19. And what is carved on the bullet?

   a. McCavern's name
   b. Arthur's name
   c. A black hand

20. Who did Mosley meet when he was in Rome?

   a. Mr Changretta
   b. Mr Carlito
   c. Mr Mussolini

SERIES FIVE:
EPISODE FOUR

Business always seems to come first in the circles Tommy moves in, even if (or perhaps because) there's been fighting, killing and all manner of nastiness beforehand. Seems the lure of the pound – particularly in light of the Wall Street Crash – is irresistible. There's kidnap and negotiation at the same time, while the Shelby women stand up to be counted for good or for ill. How much Mosley knows about all the intrigue is impossible to tell, but he's a man who seems to always know more than he lets on.

1. McCavern says his white flag is a sign of truce, while Tommy's is... what?
   a. Surrender
   b. Truth
   c. War

2. For how much is the cheque?
   a. £100
   b. £1,000
   c. £500

3. How much cash is enough for the goalkeepers?
   a. £1
   b. £10
   c. £5

4. What did Mrs Connors' husband do?
   a. Got drunk and broke all the windows
   b. Got drunk and killed her three goldfinches
   c. Got drunk and left her for a man

5. How much had the Shelbys made on the football that week?
   a. £100
   b. £1,000
   c. £10,000

6. What does Brilliant Chang have?
   a. Pure cocaine
   b. Pure opium
   c. Pure cannabis

7. How much in weight of the answer above came off the boat?
   a. Five tonnes
   b. Six tonnes
   c. Seven tonnes

8. For where is the opium shipment destined?
   a. Los Angeles
   b. San Diego
   c. San Francisco

9. And how much is that cargo worth?
   a. £1 million
   b. £500,000
   c. £250,000

10. As part of the deal to let McCavern live (for the time being), what else will happen?
   a. Aberama and Polly will get married
   b. Aberama will get a passage to New York
   c. Tommy will step down from Parliament

11. What's the name of the ballet?
   a. *The Nutcracker Suite*
   b. *Swan Lake*
   c. *Lakeside Magic*

12. Oswald says to Tommy that they are two men for whom … what … is forbidden?
   a. Extramarital affairs
   b. Forbidding
   c. Drunkenness

13. Tommy reveals where he was born, but where?
   a. In a foundling hospital called St Anne's
   b. In the bed of his dying mother
   c. On a barge called *The January*

14. Ada tells Tommy to throw what away?
   a. His opium
   b. His whisky
   c. His gun

15. Who was in the same business as Michael is being invited to take charge of?
   a. His cousin
   b. Al Capone
   c. His father

16. Who does Tommy want to guarantee the cheque?
   a. Mr Chang
   b. Mr Mosley
   c. Mr Churchill

17. How much could the company make per year, and how much for Michael per year?
    a. £3 million and £1 million
    b. £500,000 and £250,000
    c. £10 million and £5 million

18. What are the 'maids' wearing?
    a. Bells
    b. Name tags
    c. Black bonnets

19. Mosley says Tommy is a perfect balance of two gods. Which ones?
    a. Mars and Venus
    b. Apollo and Zeus
    c. Dionysus and Apollo

20. Spoiler alert: someone shoots Linda. But who?
    a. Arthur
    b. Lizzie
    c. Polly

NED DENNEHY

Charlie Strong is just that – a steady presence in the lives of the Shelbys. While he's known as Uncle Charlie, he doesn't necessarily have an actual family connection other than being a trusted confidante, insider and part of the close-knit wider group. Tommy et al. wouldn't change him for the world. He's played with relish by experienced actor Ned Dennehy, so let's have a squizz at Ned's work outside of Blinders *and see how much we know about him.*

1. In what decade was Ned born?
   a. 1950s
   b. 1960s
   c. 1970s

2. And which country is he from?
   a. Wales
   b. Ireland
   c. Scotland

3. In the late 1990s, he was a dark magic-wielding baddie in a fantasy series set in a mythical version of Irish history. Can you name the series?

   a. *Mystic Knights of Tir Na Nog*
   b. *The Mabinogion*
   c. *Brigid and the Morrigan*

4. Tougher still: name his evil fairy character.

   a. Moider
   b. Mither
   c. Mider

5. One of Ned's early appearances on film was 'Man With Roses' in Guy Ritchie's *Sherlock Holmes* (2009). He also had a blink-and-you'll-miss-it part in which 2010 blockbuster, directed by David Yates? (Clue: It's *Part I* of two hugely successful fantasy movies in a popular series). If it helps (which it won't), he's billed as 'Scared Man'.

   a. *Dune: Uprising*
   b. *Kill Bill*
   c. *Harry Potter and the Deathly Hallows*

6. Which Dickens character did Ned portray in 2015/16's TV series, *Dickensian*?

   a. Ebeneezer Scrooge
   b. Ebeneezer Goode
   c. Oliver Twist

7. The fantastic Irish Western TV series *An Klondike* was set during the Klondike Gold Rush, tracking three prospector brothers. Ned won an Irish Film and Television Academy award for playing which part?

   a. Jacob Hopkins
   b. Captain Pat Galvin
   c. Major Charles Buckeridge

8. As which name was that series known internationally?

   a. *Yabby Creek*
   b. *Darkbone Creek*
   c. *Dominion Creek*

9. The two stars of this show are David Tennant and Michael Sheen. Ned was the Duke of Hell, Hastur in several episodes. Name the series.

   a. *Anansi Story*
   b. *Good Omens*
   c. *Guards! Guards!*

10. Hastur is an evil entity in the Cthulhu Mythos, created by which legendary horror author?

   a. H.P. Lovecraft
   b. O. Henry
   c. Edgar Allan Poe

SERIES FIVE:
EPISODE FIVE

In the aftermath of the shooting, Mosley takes to the stage to show his true colours to the assembled revellers; it seems he has a receptive audience, too. If Tommy's going to be involved with the new political party, though, he'll have to make sure there's no more violence – visibly, at least. But will Tommy's information about Mosley to his secret paymasters be heeded anyway? He also goes to visit an old war friend and offers him first a way out of his agony and then one last job.

1. On which part of her body was Linda shot?
   a. Her left leg
   b. Her left arm
   c. Her right arm

2. Why did Polly bring some opium?
    a. To celebrate the wedding proposal
    b. To dose Oswald Mosley's drink
    c. In case of any little accidents

3. What does Aberama want from Arthur?
    a. To kill his enemies
    b. To be his best man
    c. To look after his horse

4. Indian cotton mills, Asian cotton mills – created with the money of Britain, but used to destroy… where, according to Mosley?
    a. Manchester and Leeds
    b. Lancashire and Yorkshire
    c. Scotland and Ireland

5. Finally, gloves off, Mosley reveals that he thinks British statesmen who are mad would follow those policies, or the servants of… what?
    a. Jewish finance
    b. American revolution
    c. Corrupt politicians

6. Mosley reckons his message can be summarised in just two words. But what are they?

   a. People power
   b. Equal rights
   c. Britain first

7. And the name of this new political party will be?

   a. British Union of Fascists
   b. British Socialist Party
   c. Britain's Last Resort

8. Mosley plans to divide the country into three areas. Who will be in the north, and therefore also controlling the racecourses to the north of Wincanton?

   a. Oswald himself
   b. Johnny Dogs
   c. Jimmy McCavern

9. What will be the job of the various regional controllers, including Tommy in the Midlands?

   a. Bringing back profits as soon as possible to add to the war chest
   b. Breaking demonstrations up and the control of rallies
   c. Working against the police and spying on soldiers

10. Why does Lizzie think Tommy is working against Mosley?
   a. To make sure the Shelbys are always in the political conversation
   b. Because someone should stop Mosley and it's the right thing to do
   c. In order to bolster the company's international export business

11. What does Arthur say he and Linda can do?
   a. Leave before light and never come back
   b. Head to the New World and start again
   c. Take out Tommy and lead the family

12. Where is Younger to be relocated?
   a. To a 'black and coloured' desk in Johannesburg
   b. To the strike action team in London
   c. To the House of Lords

13. According to Tommy, Ada's opinions of him are always wrong because they are... what?
   a. Naive
   b. Lies
   c. Hopeful

14. But what happens to Ben Younger?
    a. His car explodes and he dies
    b. He escapes to New York
    c. He drops Tommy in it

15. Not just Ben dies, tragically, but who else?
    a. Ada
    b. A 10-year-old boy
    c. Cyril the dog

16. Who is trying to hijack the shipment?
    a. The Lees
    b. The police
    c. The Titanic boys

17. What is Isiah's task?
    a. To find out who was behind the trickery
    b. To burn the policeman's body
    c. To go undercover in the police force

18. Who does Tommy go to visit?
    a. Brian
    b. Barney
    c. Barry

19. On which day will Tommy bust him out of the asylum?

a. Wednesday
b. Thursday
c. Friday

20. Tommy says he had more complex strategies in mind for Oswald Mosley, until the latter did what?

a. Spoke badly to Lizzie
b. Turned to Fascism
c. Swore at his child

SERIES FIVE:
EPISODE SIX

Winston Churchill himself gives Tommy instructions in this blockbuster series finale, with a dark foreshadowing that another war may be on the horizon. He also lets on that there is a rat in the camp, and one that is spreading information about Shelby activities to their enemies. Michael tells Tommy that the Peaky Blinders brand is sullied across the pond. There's an unexpected coda by someone previously thought dead and gone, and Tommy's plans look to bring him back on top again. However, he can't win them all... or can he?

1. What kind of whisky does Tommy prefer?
   a. Irish
   b. Scotch
   c. Japanese

2. How does Tommy define someone 'better than him'?
   a. According to their birth certificate
   b. They must prove it to him
   c. There is nobody on earth that qualifies

3. Churchill is surprised that Tommy reads what?
   a. Latin matins
   b. Hansard history
   c. Greek literature

4. What's the name of the referee of the Liverpool game that Billy managed to get to?
   a. Georgie Cambrian
   b. Harold French
   c. Lloyd Bridges

5. According to Billy, what do he and Finn only ever talk about?
   a. Football and women
   b. Football and cocaine
   c. Cocaine and hookers

6. Where is Barney?
   a. In The Garrison getting drunk as a skunk
   b. Tied to a lamppost with three Lee boys guarding him
   c. Tied in a boat with three Blinders at gunpoint

7. Michael's tail is up again. He proposes a restructuring of the company. He will be managing director, and who will be his non-executive chairman?

a. Tommy
b. Arthur
c. Finn

8. But it won't be under their real name – who would the chairman be registered as?

a. A dead man called Mr Smith
b. A dead man called Mr Jones
c. A dead man called Mr Tickle

9. After Michael's unpopular proposal is firmly knocked back and all the Shelbys leave, what's Gina's gnomic utterance?

a. That they'll have to rethink this whole strategy
b. That the Peaky Blinders always come up trumps
c. That they'll have to take the second option

10. Who trained Barney as a sniper?

a. The RAF
b. The Paratroopers
c. The Royal Marines

11. And what will Barney's task be?
    a. To kill Mosley
    b. To kill Moss
    c. To kill Aberama

12. Who will be running security for the event?
    a. Aberama Gold
    b. Jimmy McCavern
    c. Arthur Shelby

13. When the plan is enacted, all the Birmingham police will rush there, giving an opportunity to do what?
    a. Get the opium boat to Stourbridge locks
    b. Get the opium boat down to London
    c. Sink the opium boat and steal the money

14. What has Micky been doing?
    a. Passing information to the highest bidder
    b. Spying against the Lees
    c. Working with Polly and Aberama

15. What ironic word is on the doorstep of the miraculously resurrected Alfie?
    a. Lethe
    b. Welcome
    c. Leave

16. Since when, Alfie asks reasonably, did Tommy ever need an explanation for trouble? Tommy's reply…

  a. Since he entered politics
  b. Since Alfie was dead
  c. Since Mosley came on the scene

17. Charlie reveals two things about Tommy's mother. Firstly, that she drowned by suicide, and secondly… what?

  a. That she was a police informant
  b. That Charlie was in love with her
  c. That Tommy's father pushed her

18. She said that gypsies made the nails that were used in the cross of Jesus, and that's why they're cursed and restless. You have to move around or… what?

  a. The guilt catches up with you
  b. You'll take root where you stand
  c. You will never find the truth

19. What's Barney's cue to take his shot?

  a. Tommy checking his pocket watch
  b. Tommy waving at him
  c. Mosley saying the word 'Jews'

20. At the end of the episode, we see Tommy walking towards... what?

a. A vision of his mother walking into the canal. Tommy aims a gun at her
b. A vision of Grace and a black horse. Tommy puts a gun to his head
c. A vision of his mother and father together. Tommy falls to his knees and prays

SERIES FIVE: SOUNDTRACK

Surely Peaky Blinders *has the greatest soundtrack of any series, ever? Surely if Series Five is anything to go by it's got a real shout to being the best-sounding programme? We can't control those awards, unfortunately, but we can dig right into a bunch of tracks spanning literal decades of awesome sounds. Starting with…*

1. This band are sometimes credited with inventing Heavy Metal. We're not gonna debate the ins and outs of that, but we are going to ask for the Brummie outfit's name, please.
   a. Deep Purple
   b. Black Sabbath
   c. Led Zeppelin

2. One of their tracks is 'The Wizard' – we'll tell you that for free. It won't help you, though, cause we're asking you to complete the name of the other one we hear: 'War …'?
   a. Games
   b. Pigs
   c. Jackie

3. This band shares the name of their track with a later song by comedian Russ Abbot. What's the name of the group, and the name of that song? Two points on offer here.
   a. Joy Division: 'Atmosphere'
   b. New Order: 'Blue Monday'
   c. Altered Images: 'Happy Birthday'

4. Who the hell is Russ Abbot?
   a. That's showbiz
   b. That's showbiz
   c. This is a terrible joke

5. This sport-named band are heard with their song 'Love U 2 Death'. Who are they?
   a. The Pool
   b. LaCrosse
   c. The Darts

6. Anna Calvi covers 'Lady Grinning Soul', a 1973 song by which British musician?
   a. David Bowie
   b. Marc Bolan
   c. Mick Jones

7. Probably the toughest question in this book: by which American soul singer was that track originally inspired?

   a. Diana Ross
   b. Tina Turner
   c. Claudia Lennear

8. Calvi again. She performs a version of 'Ain't No Grave', which is sometimes known as 'Gonna Hold This Body Down'. Either way, it's a gospel/ blues standard. In fact, Johnny Cash recorded it on one of his Rick Rubin-produced late career albums. Which one?

   a. *American Recordings*
   b. *American VI: Ain't No Grave*
   c. *American V: Hold This Body*

9. In which 1967 Paul Newman film does a version of that song appear, this time performed by Harry Dean Stanton?

   a. *Cool Hand Luke*
   b. *The Hustler*
   c. *Paris Blues*

10. 'Never Trust A Man With A Perm' is sound advice from which Bristolian rock/punk band?

   a. Massive Attack
   b. Katzenmusik
   c. Idles

PEAKY WHISPERS

You Will Need: Pen and paper (though this is optional)

How to Play: The youngest person in the group thinks of a quote from *Peaky Blinders*. In their best Small Heath accent, they whisper the phrase *once only* into the ear of the person sitting on their left. That person then repeats it to the person sitting on their own left (everyone must use their best *Peaky* accent), and so on around the table/room.

Meanwhile, the youngest person writes the quote on a piece of paper and writes down the phrase, making sure nobody else can see it. The final person in the group says the phrase out loud, in their own best Brummie voice, and the youngest holds up the real phrase on their piece of paper. How far away from the original has the phrase become? If you're not using pen and paper, the original phrase-sayer merely repeats the original quote out loud.

This game is sometimes called 'Telephone' or 'Chinese Whispers' and even though it seems simple, it ain't half hilarious as the night goes on!

Variation: The final phrase is marked out of 10 points by all players, who analyse how close it is (or isn't) to the original. This becomes the score of the original phrase-sayer. Play as many rounds as there are people in the room, with the job of phrase-whisperer moving one place to the left each time so that everyone gets a go. Whoever gets the most points wins – and whoever gets the least points has to undertake a forfeit chosen by their fellow players.

Forfeit suggestions:

* Take off one shoe for the rest of the evening
* Go and wash up immediately
* Buy everybody a 1924 Bentley 6.5 Litre Vanden Plas
* Talk like Elvis/Yoda/Cardi B for the next hour
* Every time someone asks them a question, they must answer in rhyme…

…we're sure you can think of oodles more, so over to you!

SERIES SIX

SERIES SIX: EPISODE ONE

We left Tommy on the brink of ending it all. But, of course, that wouldn't be a great start to another series, would it? We do, however, say goodbye to three characters – including the matriarch Polly Shelby aka Elizabeth Gray. The loss of such a powerful, mystical presence to the Shelby family is yet to be fully realised, but one of Tommy's main restraining forces is now no longer present. Sadly, the actress Helen McCrory who delivered such an incredible performance as Polly passed away in real life, and this episode is beautifully dedicated to her.

1. Tommy *did* pull the trigger to kill himself, but the gun was empty. How so?
   a. He'd picked up the wrong gun on his way out of the house
   b. Arthur took the bullets out when Tommy was throwing up
   c. The gun was a decoy that he kept just to make sure

2. Tommy talks to his mother; she was allowed to pass through to the other side, but he was not. Why?
   a. As if there were to be (he says) another consequence
   b. As if there were to be (he says) a retribution
   c. As if there were to be (he says) a war of finality

3. The phone rings. The caller says that it was they who foiled Tommy's operation. But who are they?
   a. The UVF
   b. The IRA
   c. The UDA

4. Watching the funeral pyre, who vows to take revenge on Tommy?
   a. Michael
   b. Arthur
   c. Linda

5. We pick up the action several years later. Where are we and Tommy now?
   a. Miquelon Island, French Newfoundland
   b. Vancouver Island, French Columbia
   c. Toronto Port, French Ontario

6. We see Michael. What's different about his appearance?
   a. He's got long hair and wears sunglasses
   b. He's grown a moustache and wears a fedora
   c. He's in jeans, a T-shirt and a waistcoat

7. What does Tommy order to drink, to the surprise/disgust of the patrons in the bar?
   a. Malibu
   b. Water
   c. Gin

8. What is the headline in the newspaper?
   a. Canada is independent as of midnight
   b. Whisky is outlawed as of midnight
   c. Prohibition ends at midnight

9. An angry man tries to make Tommy raise a glass of whisky to the people of Miquelon. What's the man's name?
   a. Jean-Luc
   b. Jean-Claude
   c. Jean-Jeanée

10. There's a projector. It's a gift from Hollywood! But from whom, specifically?
   a. Buster Keaton
   b. Harold Lloyd
   c. Charlie Chaplin

11. Where are Lizzie, Charles and Ruby going to go?
    a. On a ship to Canada to meet Tommy
    b. On a plane to Norway to see Santa
    c. On a boat to Wolverhampton docks

12. Why is Miquelon such a useful island to Tommy's, and possibly Michael's, new venture?
    a. It lies outside territorial waters
    b. It is heavily fortified
    c. It is controlled by the Mafia

13. How much has Tommy offered his comrade in the Préfet des Gendarmes to allow the Boston-Miquelon boats to keep running?
    a. One million Francs
    b. £500,000
    c. Twelve million Francs

14. Who is Uncle Jack?
    a. Gina's uncle
    b. Arthur's uncle
    c. Lizzie's uncle

15. Who is the author of the poem Tommy recites in his meeting with Michael et al.?
    a. John Donne
    b. William Blake
    c. William Wordsworth

16. By what does Tommy say that the informant could be identified?
   a. A black hand tattooed on his chest with the word 'Danger'
   b. A red hand tattooed on his torso with the word 'Fealty'
   c. A bleeding heart tattoo with 'Maria', the letters in red

17. Which name does Tommy give to the police when he phones to inform on Michael?
   a. Aberama Gold
   b. Grace Dream
   c. Mr Jones

18. Which impressive figure does Gina say Uncle Jack is on his way to meet with?
   a. The President of the United States
   b. Winston Churchill
   c. The President of Canada

19. If Jack does not take the deal, with whom will Tommy be dealing?
   a. The East Boston Jews
   b. The West Boston Italians
   c. The North Boston Irish

20. What has Ruby been saying in her delirium?
    a. Tickna mora o'beng
    b. The Devil will meet the Lord
    c. Do not trust the dark ones

SERIES SIX:
EPISODE TWO

Tommy just cannot resist the lure of shenanigans, can he? He's still trying to play several sides off each other, including his old 'mate' Oswald Mosley; but is Mosley still the only one that he can't find a way to beat? Sickness is also to the fore, with Tommy suffering, as well as someone younger who seems to have inherited Polly's second sight – though it's all very portentous. Arthur Shelby's also in a bad way – can he be saved from himself, the needle and the damage done? In fact, can anyone at all be saved?

1. What's the name of the doctor that Tommy takes Ruby to see?
    a. Dr Robert
    b. Dr Whiteley
    c. Dr Stephen

2. Lizzie tells Tommy he talks as if he's doing what?
   a. Ready to meet his maker
   b. Watching everything on a screen
   c. Never seen her before

3. How long has it been since Tommy has had a drink?
   a. Seven hours and fifteen days
   b. Six years, two months and a day
   c. Four years, one month and six days

4. What happens to Tommy in the bathroom?
   a. He falls asleep in the bath
   b. He has a seizure
   c. He locks himself in

5. When does he say the Peaky Blinders will rest?
   a. After the Boston deal is done
   b. After the Americans pull out
   c. After the Canada deal is done

6. There will be a rally that Saturday. Where?
   a. The Houses of Parliament
   b. The Bull Ring market
   c. West Bromwich

7. Who's the lady in the beret?
   a. Laura McKee of the IRA
   b. Maureen McCue of the UVF
   c. Jemima McCavern of the Billy Boys

8. What does Tommy say is a good name for a racehorse?
   a. Spineless crusader
   b. Ethical quandary
   c. Moral turpitude

9. One of the letters is from a very important person. Who is it?
   a. The Prime Minister
   b. The President of the United States of America
   c. Winston Churchill

10. Why is Uncle Jack really coming to London?
   a. To suss out how strong the Fascist movement is in Britain
   b. To check on the state of the Blinders' standing army
   c. To set up some new cocaine-selling opportunities

11. By being in among the Fascists, what does Tommy reckon he can do?
   a. Change them
   b. Undermine them
   c. Expel them

12. What does Alfie say the sound of a tenor giving it everything reminds him of?
   a. The sound of the mortars as they fell around him
   b. The sound of heaven enticing him towards his cloud
   c. Italians crying out as he thrust his bayonet into them

13. What would Tommy take in return if Alfie's family bought the opium?
   a. A credit note for six million dollars
   b. Warehouses in Camden
   c. The rum distillery

14. And what would Tommy use that for?
   a. To buy out Johnny Dogs finally
   b. He would build houses for the needy
   c. He would make it into an enormous woodyard

15. What explanation does Tommy offer the reporter who asks why he, a socialist, would go to a rally of Fascists?
   a. He says he must always keep an eye on what is happening
   b. He says Mosley was once socialist, and that the constituencies border each other
   c. He says he does not believe Mosley is actually a Fascist

16. What's wrong with what an addled Arthur is wearing?
    a. He has a black shirt on, which is the colour of Mosley's Fascists
    b. He has not tied his waistcoat on properly, so it looks ridiculous
    c. He is wearing denim, which is the uniform of the plebs

17. What deal does Tommy offer Arthur?
    a. That he will be back in the family if he kills Mosley
    b. That if he is clean and sober for two weeks, he will write to Linda
    c. That if he leaves for America immediately, he will receive £100,000

18. Where do Tommy and Jack meet?
    a. In a church
    b. In the boatyard
    c. By the canal

19. Who is coming for Ruby and Tommy?
    a. The tall man
    b. The grey man
    c. The white lady

20. Who does Tommy phone at the end of the episode?
    a. Esme
    b. Mosley
    c. Ada

NATASHA O'KEEFFE

To play the second wife of Tommy requires an actor of exceptional emotional range, and thus Lizzie Stark is in excellent hands under the expert skills of Natasha O'Keeffe. When we delve into her career, we can see everything from growing TV success to quite a few movies, as well as more than one music video. Clearly, the story is just beginning for this talented performer, so let's have a good squizz at her career to date and see how well we know Natasha herself.

1. Natasha's parents are from County Cavan in Northern Ireland, but where was she born?
   a. Cavan
   b. Brighton
   c. Cardiff

2. Tough one, but if you know it you know it: what's Natasha's full name?

a. Natasha Dervill O'Keeffe
b. Natasha Orville O'Keeffe
c. Natasha O'Keeffe-Shelby

3. Her first big TV break was in a BBC Scotland show tracking the lives of a group of gay women in the Glasgow area. It ran for two series on BBC Three, in 2010 and 2012. What was the name of the show?

a. *Glaswegian Girls*
b. *Let Us Be*
c. *Lip Service*

4. And her character's name?

a. Cat MacKenzie
b. Tess Roberts
c. Sadie Anderson

5. Unfortunately, that show was cancelled before a third series could be made. Undeterred, Natasha went on to portray Abbey Smith in a well-loved black comedy/sci-fi drama about offenders who gained special powers. But what was it called?

a. *Black Flag*
b. *Mekons*
c. *Misfits*

6. It ran for five series. In which two seasons did Natasha feature?
   a. One and Two
   b. Three and Four
   c. Four and Five

7. Let's talk about those music videos now. First, in 2008, Natasha was seen as a dissolute, out-of-control member of a royal family.. We'll even give you the name of the track: 'Falling Down'. Do you know which band's single it was?
   a. Blur
   b. Oasis
   c. Pulp

8. From Britpop to indie-folk-shoegaze, and in 2015 she was in a video for which band? This time, the single was called 'Numbers' and the album was called *Not to Disappear*. Come on, that's enough clues: what's the band called?
   a. Daughter
   b. Son
   c. Cousin

9. Like many of her *Peaky Blinders* compadres, Natasha's appeared in a show about which fictional Victorian detective?

  a. Sherlock Holmes
  b. John Watson
  c. Loveday Brooke

10. And that character was the brainchild of which author?

  a. Arthur Shelby
  b. Arthur Conan Doyle
  c. Philip Marlowe

11. Natasha grew up in Tooting, but went to a different country to study her craft. What was the name of her college?

  a. Scotland Academy of Dramatic Arts
  b. Finland Drama College
  c. Royal Welsh College of Music and Drama

12. She played a character in this movie, based on a once-thought-unfilmable novel by Scottish writer Irvine Welsh. Which film was it?

  a. *Trainspotting*
  b. *Trainspotting II*
  c. *Filth*

13. More grimy, dark Victorian stuff on the small screen during late 2015 for Natasha. Her character was called Fedora in this one, an ITV single-series drama about which doctor and his evil alter ego?

a. *Holmes and Watson*
b. *Jekyll and Hyde*
c. *Marc and Frankie*

14. Which one-time *Fast Show* performer and writer was responsible for writing that show?

a. Mark Williams
b. Charlie Higson
c. Caroline Aherne

15. A crime drama based on books by Robert Galbraith, now. Natasha's character, Charlotte Campbell, is a regular in this six-season telly feast. Simply name the series.

a. *Strike*
b. *Spare*
c. *Gutterball*

16. Galbraith is listed as writer of the books – but which mega-famous person was revealed as the actual author?

a. J.R. Hartley
b. J.K. Rowling
c. J.P.R. Williams

17. Into Space now, and Natasha's character Emma Grieves was once a renowned scientist but is now in prison for her rebellious acts. It was on Sky One in 2021. What's the series?

a. *Interstellar*
b. *Intergalactic*
c. *Interfrastic*

18. Can you name that prison transport ship?

a. *Hemlock*
b. *Tardis*
c. *Galacticus*

19. Natasha was in the second and third series of this fantasy-drama Amazon Prime Video broadcast, which aired between 2021 and 2025. It's got reincarnation, primordial evil, mysterious powers and mystical dreams all over the shop. Based on a series of books of the same name by Robert Jordan, what's the show called?

a. *Conan the Barbarian*
b. *Conehead the Librarian*
c. *The Wheel of Time*

20. Back to the silver screen… A period drama and an adaptation of a true story about a family champagne business, beginning in the late 1700s. What's the name of this 2023 movie?

a. *Dom Perignon*
b. *Widow Clicquot*
c. *Mumm-Ra*

SERIES SIX:
EPISODE THREE

Tommy Shelby straddles so many worlds it's a wonder he's not developed saddle sores. Will he be able to save the stricken Ruby? Or are there more mysterious forces at work, ones that even his incredible chess-game mind cannot find a way to turn to his advantage? Ada, meanwhile, is tasked with keeping an important meeting on track. There's trouble in Liverpool and Arthur's condition is as precarious as it's ever been. Will people use it to take advantage?

1. What is wrong with Ruby?
   a. She has consumption
   b. She has broken ribs
   c. She has the vapours

2. To what does Tommy compare himself in his apology to the medical staff?
   a. A crab in a bucket
   b. A horse in a crate
   c. A dog in a manger

3. If collapsing the lung doesn't work, what will the doctors try?
   a. Gold salts
   b. Silver salts
   c. Diamond salts

4. How many days of Ada's time does Tommy request?
   a. Seven
   b. Three
   c. Five

5. Nancy Mitford says she doesn't read novels. What does she read?
   a. Pornography and politics
   b. Newspapers and comics
   c. Magazines and catalogues

6. When it's time for what Nancy calls The Great Cleansing, her odious comment is that she'll argue for the Jews to be 'dealt with', but... what?

   a. The Blacks to be spared
   b. The Scottish to be slaves
   c. The gypsies to be spared

7. Gina told Jack that the Shelbys speak with the dead because they are...?

   a. Wizards and thieves
   b. Tramps and gypsies
   c. Witches and sorcerers

8. To what disease did a young Nelson lose a brother and sister?

   a. Black lung
   b. Consumption
   c. The vapours

9. Ada invites Nelson and Mosley to a meeting at Tommy's house. To meet whom, and to discuss what?

   a. Churchill and the future of Scotland
   b. Someone from Ireland and the future of Europe
   c. The King and the upcoming horseracing season

10. Where is Arthur?
    a. Locked in the cash safe
    b. Locked in The Garrison bar
    c. Locked in the bedroom

11. What's the name of the union organiser who's stealing opium up in Liverpool?
    a. Hayden Christensen
    b. Hayden Stagg
    c. Barry Stagg

12. For how long has Arthur been clean?
    a. A week
    b. A month
    c. Ten days

13. From where has Isiah recruited his cousins for the mission?
    a. The mean streets of Wolverhampton
    b. The streets of Alum Rock
    c. The docklands of Manchester

14. What euphemism for a death sentence do the Peaky Blinders use with Hayden?
    a. A one-way ticket on the downstairs express
    b. Sweet release from the bleak midwinter
    c. A visit to the Black Star pub

15. Hayden tells Arthur that Jesus, Arthur's wife and Arthur's kids can't help him. Who can?

a. Hayden can set him straight
b. Only Tommy can do this
c. Arthur himself is the only one

16. What does Arthur do which is out of character, after Hayden's speech?

a. He stands the lads down and they leave
b. He lets the others lead the beating
c. He curses God and Jesus to Hell

17. Stephen Graham is an absolutely boss dodgy bloke, isn't he?

a. Yeah, in everything he's in
b. Not bad for a small Scouser
c. Aye, he's a beast of an actor

18. Tommy says he lost his mind a long time ago, so what does he use?

a. The crate it came in
b. The horsebox of his heart
c. Memories of better days

19. To whom did Bethany Barwell give the stone, and what happened?

a. Her sister Evadne, who put it around the neck of a daughter – who died that night, age seven
b. A cursed cousin, who has gone insane and is on the rampage somewhere up north
c. Her mother, who started seeing visions of black horses on the horizon

20. Esme says she'll put out the word that Tommy's is looking for Evadne Barwell to lift the curse. What payment does Esme want?

a. Ten thousand pounds
b. Gold
c. Silver

SERIES SIX:
EPISODE FOUR

Funerals, retribution, long-lost kids… it's all happening in Tommy Shelby's world. Dark clouds are gathering in the wider political arena, and Tommy's finding it ever more difficult to reconcile his undercover plans with the people he must deal with. Is it all too much even for him to bear? The rage is never far from the surface but will he be able to hold it together at all? He and Arthur share some honest truths, salving his soul a little – but a bombshell medical issue may yet send him over the edge.

1. Who does Tommy ask to read the eulogy – but that person cannot do so?
    a. Arthur
    b. Isiah
    c. Michael

2. In Ruby's memory, what does Tommy pledge they will do with whatever comes down the river?
   a. Make it peaceful, honest and good, and send it on better than it was
   b. Make it full of joy, worthy and sell it for the highest prize
   c. Send it on without touching, messing or thieving

3. Who or what does Tommy tell Evadne he is present on behalf of?
   a. The police
   b. The Peaky Blinders
   c. The blue sapphire

4. What does he give to Esme?
   a. A bag of diamonds
   b. A bag of gold dust
   c. A bag of money

5. What is the name of the girl that Esme reveals Tommy slept with at Appleby Fair, before going to France?
   a. Sandra
   b. Zelda
   c. Zamma

6. Under which kind of tree did they do the deed?
   a. Hazel
   b. Oak
   c. Larch

7. There was a boy born with the same colour eyes as the tree's name. What's his name and where is he?
   a. Duke, at the fairgrounds
   b. Dirk, in the police
   c. Dan, in the army

8. Tommy tells Lizzie there will be a new fund. What will it research?
   a. Corruption in the armed forces
   b. Causes of and cures for consumption
   c. The nature of human anger and revenge

9. In the cellar, what does Tommy finally realise about Arthur?
   a. That he's always been more than a tunneller
   b. That Arthur let him win a fight as a kid
   c. That Arthur is a lover, not a fighter

10. What's the line number in the long black tunnel on the Dudley canal?
   a. Line number one
   b. Line number two
   c. Line number three

11. Which cars are there, as reported by young Charles?
   a. A Porsche and a Lamborghini
   b. A Ford and a Volvo
   c. A Bentley and a Rolls-Royce

12. At Tommy's house, waiting for him to come downstairs, Diana tells the others that she went to a similar meeting in Berlin. Who was there?
   a. Hitler, Goering, Himmler
   b. Dönitz, Heinrich, Hess
   c. Goebbels, Himmler, Hassler

13. Who has the ear of the President of the United States of America?
   a. Oswald Mosley
   b. Tommy Shelby
   c. Jack Nelson

14. What does Tommy have to do to prove to his guests that he's one of them?
   a. Make a Nazi salute and say 'Perish Judah'
   b. Cut himself on the arm with a swastika
   c. Stand up and denounce Arthur as a Communist

15. What does Ada reveal to Karl?
   a. That his dad was from Wales
   b. That his dad was Jewish
   c. That his dad was a Lee

16. As a result of Tommy 'proving' himself, what does Jack grant him?
    a. The freedom of New York City
    b. The ability to move to California undetected
    c. The ability to sell his 'merchandise' into Boston

17. What did Tommy burn?
    a. Mosley's suit
    b. Ruby's chair
    c. Charles' toy horse

18. Who does Tommy catch sleeping with Mosley?
    a. Gina
    b. Ada
    c. Lizzie

19. And what is Tommy's job for her as a result?
    a. To shadow Mosley in Berlin and report back
    b. To tell him everything Michael does
    c. To go immediately away and never come back

20. How long does the doctor say Tommy has left to live?
    a. Ten years, maybe twenty
    b. A year, maybe eighteen months
    c. Three years, maybe four

BENJAMIN ZEPHANIAH

Street preacher, father of Isiah, friend of Tommy since serving with him in the war, that's Jeremiah 'Jimmy' Jesus. We encounter him ploughing his own furrow throughout the show and he's one of the more interesting supporting characters to consider. The person playing Jimmy, though, is renowned for way more than his acting skills: he was also a poet, musician, professor and writer. It's the incomparable Benjamin Zephaniah, who sadly ascended from this plane in 2023. Let's have a look at his career, on and off screen.

1. How many honorary doctorates did Benjamin receive over his lifetime?
    a. 20
    b. 10
    c. None

2. In which city was he born?
   a. Liverpool
   b. Birmingham
   c. Slough

3. From which geographical area had his parents originated?
   a. The Caribbean
   b. America
   c. Asia

4. Zephaniah is rightly feted as one of the greatest poets the UK has ever produced. But why was he unable to make a mark at his Birmingham school, Broadway?
   a. He couldn't read or write due to undiagnosed dyslexia
   b. He was caught fighting with his classmates too often
   c. He was a regular truant and nobody could find him

5. Benjamin had a tough upbringing, and spent time in prison. For what?
   a. Assault
   b. Burglary
   c. Possession

6. He began writing about his experiences on the streets, including much overt racism. His first book was published in 1980. What's the title?
   a. *Pen Rhythm*
   b. *Writing Fierce*
   c. *Rasta Rhyme*

7. With which legendary reggae group did he work on his debut 1982 album, *Rasta*?
   a. The Beat
   b. The Wailers
   c. Steel Pulse

8. As a result of a song on that album, he eventually met which towering African figure?
   a. Thomas Sankara
   b. Nelson Mandela
   c. Kwame Nkrumah

9. What was the name of his 1999 debut novel, published by Bloomsbury?
   a. *Race*
   b. *Time*
   c. *Face*

10. To which religion was Benjamin affiliated?
   a. Christianity
   b. Rastafarianism
   c. Judaism

11. In 2009, there was a poll run by the BBC which asked the nation to vote for its favourite poet. Zephaniah placed third. Who were the top two?
   a. R.S. Thomas and Dylan Thomas
   b. Virginia Woolf and D.H. Lawrence
   c. T.S. Eliot and John Donne

12. Which honour, for which he was recommended by Tony Blair, did Zephaniah turn down in 2003?
   a. MBE
   b. OBE
   c. CBE

13. He was an animal rights campaigner among many other activisms. Which food body was he an honorary patron of?
   a. The Vegetarian Society
   b. Health for All
   c. The Vegan Society

14. When Benjamin appeared on *Desert Island Discs* in 1997, which book did he choose?
   a. *The Poetical Works of Shelley*
   b. *Bertrand Russell's History of Philosophy*
   c. *The Anarchist Handbook*

15. What was the name of his 2018 autobiography?
   a. *Still Angry After All These Years*
   b. *The Best Words Cut The Deepest*
   c. *The Life and Rhymes of Benjamin Zephaniah*

16. In 2016, he curated an exhibition at the Southbank Centre in London. It included artwork by which usually under-represented groups?
   a. Prisoners and ex-prisoners
   b. Hospitalised artists
   c. Passers-by to the Centre

17. And what was that exhibition called?
   a. *We Are All Human*
   b. *Passing Time Creatively*
   c. *We Will Care*

18. What was the name of his debut radio play, which was a winner of 1998's BBC Young Playwrights Festival Award?

  a. *Cyclone Rhyme*
  b. *Tornado Rhythm*
  c. *Hurricane Dub*

19. Benjamin won Best Original Song in a 2008 Folk Music awards ceremony. What was the name of the track, on which he collaborated with The Imagined Village?

  a. 'Tam Lyn Retold'
  b. 'Rasta Folkie'
  c. 'Hancocks Heart'

20. Which perhaps unexpected language did he study for many years towards the end of his life?

  a. Welsh
  b. Mandarin
  c. Hungarian

SERIES SIX: EPISODE FIVE

Following his heart-to-heart with Arthur, Tommy takes extreme measures to look after his brother's health. The newest Shelby tries out a couple of jobs for size, ruffling feathers everywhere as he does. There's redemption on the cards for one Shelby brother, but Tommy begins to realise that he personally is as bad as any of the scheming lowlifes he's been dealing with. Finally, Michael has an intriguing visitor who offers him freedom in exchange for something that the estranged son of Polly has been wanting to do for a long time anyway.

1. How many pounds of opium does the shop in Chinatown still have?
    a. Four
    b. Five
    c. Six

2. There will be no more opium in which areas of Birmingham?
   a. Small Heath and Bordesley
   b. Ladywood and Digbeth
   c. Edgbaston and Erdington

3. Montague Street's trade in what Tommy calls 'powder' is now done. But by whose orders?
   a. Peaky Blinders
   b. The IRA
   c. Birmingham Urban District Council

4. What's the name of Finn's new wife?
   a. Maggie
   b. Mary
   c. Missy

5. And what is Duke's real first name?
   a. Charles
   b. Erasmus
   c. Horse

6. According to Duke, who were his parents?
   a. Duke of the Saxon Shore and a Romany Queen
   b. High Priest of Wolverhampton and the Gypsy Queen
   c. A disgraced politician and a prostitute

7. How much money does Tommy offer to Linda's foundation?
   a. £1,000
   b. £10,000
   c. £5,000

8. Linda says she will help Arthur, but she won't do… what?
   a. Sleep with him
   b. Divorce him
   c. Hurt him

9. What is engraved on the bullet that Tommy gives to Hayden Stagg?
   a. Co-ordinates to Boston
   b. Stagg's name
   c. The Shelby family logo

10. When his last bit of business is done, Tommy tells Stagg, he will be… what?
   a. A legitimate businessman
   b. An ordinary mortal man
   c. The new Prime Minister

11. To what book does Lizzie refer?
   a. Tommy's book of regrets
   b. Arthur's personal Bible
   c. Tommy's book of finance

12. When Lizzie married Tommy, she also married… what?
    a. The Shelbys
    b. A curse
    c. Birmingham

13. What's Moss's rank these days?
    a. Inspector
    b. Corporal
    c. Chief superintendent

14. What is the referee supposed to do in the forthcoming match?
    a. Give Birmingham City a penalty in the last minute
    b. Give Wolverhampton Wanderers a throw-in in the first minute
    c. Send off the Birmingham City inside-left at half-time

15. What becomes of the referee?
    a. Finn kills him
    b. Arthur kills him
    c. Billy kills him

16. Who does Isiah have to ask for at the foundry?
    a. Mr Patches
    b. Mr Scratches
    c. Mr Cavern

17. Things go from bad to worse for poor Billy. Who is next to 'persuade' him to do something for him?
   a. Jack Nelson
   b. Michael Shelby
   c. Chief Superintendent Moss

18. What's Duke's view on people?
   a. They energise him
   b. There's not enough
   c. They piss him off

19. What's the aristocracy's own way of shaking hands, according to Diana Mitford?
   a. Exchanging gold rings
   b. Sleeping with each other
   c. Taking cocaine and heroin

20. Who has Michael consulted to ask what he ought to do?
   a. The police
   b. Jack Nelson
   c. His mother

SERIES SIX:
EPISODE SIX

Is it possible for a dealer in death and violence ever to find peace? For all Thomas Shelby's dark nights of the soul and desperate wish to help his fellow humans (and horses), his personal body count of killings is enormous; let alone all those who have perished simply by coming into his blackened, destructive orbit. It's surely true that the Thomas Shelby who went to France is not the one who came back. But as he yearns for release from his personal hell, there's still business to be done, and loose ends to tie up. Is his destiny already set, though? Enjoy this bumper quiz for a bumper episode...

1. Where is Tommy off to?
   a. America
   b. Ireland
   c. Canada

2. Charles says Lizzie's not his mum, but… what?
   a. She's more his mum than Tommy is his dad
   b. She's the best woman he knows
   c. She'll always be his best friend

3. Which factory do the Peaky Blinders have a very good relationship with?
   a. The BBC warehouses in Lindbergh Avenue
   b. The BSA factory in Armoury Road
   c. The BCFCS association in Farrar Road

4. Duke says he's killed a man already. Where, when and why?
   a. A Bridgnorth hospital orderly who wouldn't let his dying mother in because she was an uninsured gypsy
   b. An Ironbridge police officer who wouldn't pick up his dying mother because she lay a curse on him
   c. An Oswestrian gun runner who wouldn't talk to his mother because she was a woman

5. What does Tommy confess to Arthur?
   a. That he's in trouble with the Chinese opium dealers
   b. That he has inoperable tuberculoma in his brain
   c. That he's been working for Churchill all this time

6. How much are the construction contracts worth?
   a. £1 million
   b. £5 million
   c. £10 million

7. How much money will Tommy be collecting in Canada?
   a. £1 million
   b. £5 million
   c. £10 million

8. Who are the only people Tommy wants to come to his funeral (burn the wagon)?
   a. Arthur, Charlie, Curly
   b. Arthur, Michael, Charles
   c. Finn, Michael, Duke

9. What does 'tachipen' mean?
   a. Trouble
   b. Truth
   c. Terror

10. Aside from cash and valuables, what items are there in the grounds of Arrow House that Tommy needs to be dealt with?
   a. Treasure chests
   b. Dead bodies
   c. Incriminating papers

11. Where will Arthur be when the 'party' in Arrow House is happening?
   a. In The Garrison drinking champagne for his anniversary
   b. On the way to Canada to collect payment with Tommy
   c. Watching the football with his good friends

12. What time does the clock strike when it is told to, as Tommy tells Finn?
   a. Midnight
   b. Midday
   c. Six

13. What's Michael's assessment of new boy Duke?
   a. He's going to be a terrible threat in the future
   b. He's not a threat
   c. He's easy to turn to their cause

14. What's written on the paper plane that Tommy throws across to Diana?
   a. Families owning land and facing foreclosure
   b. Families that have crossed the Shelbys
   c. Families that have lost relatives to war

15. Where does Tommy refuse to have sex?
  a. In the house of the Lord
  b. On the floor of Parliament
  c. On the Tory benches

16. Where are Oswald and Diana to get married?
  a. Arrow House
  b. Canada
  c. Berlin

17. How is Tommy getting to Canada?
  a. Paddle steamer
  b. Cruise ship
  c. Aeroplane

18. What does Jack call Michael, to the latter's clear annoyance?
  a. New boy
  b. Shelby the second
  c. Mickey

19. What time exactly is the car bomb set to blow?
  a. 14.30
  b. 15.50
  c. 16.20

20. Duke gives Finn the gun to shoot Billy the rat with, but what does Finn do?
    a. Tries to shoot himself twice
    b. Tries to shoot Isiah and Duke
    c. Shoots Duke and Arthur

21. As a result, what happens?
    a. Finn takes over as boss of the family
    b. Finn is banished from the Shelby family
    c. Finn is taken to hospital

22. What unusual weapon do Arthur and Jeremiah use to get rid of the IRA attackers?
    a. Mustard gas
    b. A machine gun
    c. Cluster bombs

23. What excuse does Michael give for not getting in the car with Tommy?
    a. That he's forgotten his keys
    b. That he's forgotten his cigarettes
    c. That he will not ride with a traitor

24. Michael tells Tommy that nobody can make their own choice without… what?
    a. Tommy's opinion
    b. Money in their pocket
    c. The grace of God

25. In which part of Michael's body does Tommy shoot him?
    a. In the groin
    b. In the eye
    c. In the heart

26. Who tells Tommy to put his cigarette out?
    a. Ada
    b. Arthur
    c. Alfie

27. Who dies in their bed, according to Alfie?
    a. Good people
    b. Weak people
    c. Lazy people

28. Tommy says he's made good on his promise and requisitioned the country estate to make room for working people's houses. As well as his good intentions, how many pounds of dynamite did the trick?
    a. 1,000
    b. 1,500
    c. 2,000

29. Who does he say ought to run for a seat in Parliament, should one become available?
   a. Arthur
   b. Isiah
   c. Ada

30. Tommy goes to his caravan to end his life. But what happens? This, folks, is a major spoiler, so please describe it in your own beautifully constructed words…

SERIES SIX: SOUNDTRACK

The final act/s, and to contribute to the sense of importance the music ranges from Classical to truly heart-wrenching. Some titans of the music world's tracks are included on the soundtrack, and we're left in no doubt as to the absolute heft of narrative with which they marry…

1. Time for one more cover version of that fab title music, which to remind ourselves is 'Red Right Hand' by Nick Cave and the Bad Seeds. But which legendary singer/poet/punk/icon gives us the good stuff this time?
   a. Patti Smith
   b. Debbie Harry
   c. Chrissie Hynde

2. We've even got Pavarotti this time, singing 'Nessun Dorma' alongside a boys' choir, the London Philharmonic and more. Sing it! No, actually don't do that, we'll take points away. Instead, translate 'Nessun Dorma' from Italian.
   a. 'Nissan Doormat'

b. 'Night Dreams'
c. 'None Shall Sleep'

3. So cool he transcended language entirely to name this track with numbers alone, that's Thom Yorke. But what's the song in question?
a. '4.20'
b. '69'
c. '5.17'

4. 'Lacrimosa' from Mozart's Requiem in D Minor is elegiac and gorgeously so. But never mind that, what was the name of the song by Falco featuring the composer's middle name?
a. 'Wolfgang Punk'
b. 'Rock Me Amadeus'
c. 'Rock Me Doctor Zaius'

5. Two tracks to enjoy here from a very much-missed Irish chanteuse, namely 'In This Heart' and 'Lullaby for Cain'. But which singer are we talking about?
a. Dolores O'Riordan
b. Moya Brennan
c. Sinéad O'Connor

6. Surely we all know that her most famous, and extremely emotional, song is the wonderful 'Nothing Compares 2 U', complete with the video and her single teardrop. But who wrote that song?

a. Sinéad O'Connor
b. Prince
c. Linda Perry

7. A 1950s and 1960s icon gives us 'One Silver Dollar'. Who's the singer?

a. Jayne Mansfield
b. Marilyn Monroe
c. Dusty Springfield

8. How many men are swinging, according to the title of the Count Basie track included here?

a. Six
b. Seven
c. Sixteen

9. This Cavan-born singer provides her lovely, fragile acoustic/strings track 'Blackbird'. What's her name?

a. Sinéad O'Connor
b. Lisa O'Neill
c. Andrea Corr

10. That artist also sings the song that plays over the final scene of the finale of the show. It's a Bob Dylan track from 1970's *Self Portrait*. Enough clues: which song is it?

a. 'Early Mornin' Rain'
b. 'Living The Blues'
c. 'All The Tired Horses'

FEET UP

This game can be played throughout the day/evening as you go through the quiz book/watching party. Beware: it's going to get extremely addictive. And once you start playing, well, we take no responsibility for the rest of your days in which you'll invoke this rule/game at every opportunity. The author first encountered this game at the home of his late friend, Jon Hall. Now he passes this irritating, brilliant party game on to the world at large…

How to Play: Simply, once one person takes their feet off the floor and keeps them there, everyone else must do so, silently and without letting on to anyone else. The person that's left with their feet on the floor has to make everyone else a cup of tea/go and fetch the biscuits/order fast food on the phone. Obviously, everyone has to know that this is what's at stake at the start of proceedings, so it's a good idea to play the first round early on: 'Folks, I'm going to make the first round of teas/get the cold beverages in. But the second round will have to be done by whoever is slowest getting their feet off the floor. Are we ready?'. Cue everyone rushing to lift their feet, and the slowest person therefore being next to make the tea (or whatever) after the first round.

Note: There is no 'timing' here. Once someone has had their turn making the tea (after Round One, which is the 'get to know the game' round) then it's down to them to initiate the following round. So, whoever made the tea in Round Two is in charge of taking their feet off the floor. You may, if you like, make eye contact with one of your friends/family to clue them in to what you're doing. They will probably rush to copy you, and that movement *might* mean others join in. Remember – nobody can talk about what they're doing, but just do the action.

Obviously don't do it too often – nobody wants to end up with eleven cups of tea next to them that they haven't drunk yet. It is a great way to democratise the process of, say, getting snacks in between episodes of *Peaky Blinders*, and an absolutely cracking way of getting your own back on someone who is so taken by the sound of their own voice that they're oblivious to what's going on around them.

Variation: It doesn't have to be feet, of course. You could choose to put your finger in your ear, or stick your tongue out, or anything that is physically possible for all the people who are present. It has to be something recognisable from across a possibly darkened room, though.

Last one winking their left eye has to refill the Bombay Mix, folks! Enjoy!

BY ORDER OF... WHO?: QUOTES QUIZ

Peaky Blinders *is an endlessly quotable show. Your simple task here is to match the quote with the character that actually said it. Too easy? Well, in that case we'll attribute the quotes to different characters entirely, to throw you off the scent. We've also used their maiden names where applicable, just to put another spanner in the works. Away you go...*

'Men always tell their troubles to a barmaid.'

– Lizzie Shelby

'When you're dead already, you're free.'

– Luca Changretta

'I heard you dress well, Mr Shelby. But now I see, not so well as me.'

– Aberama Gold

'There is good in my heart, but these hands belong to the Devil.'

– Polly Gray

'Men like us, Mr Shelby, will always be alone. And what love we get, we will have to pay for.'

– Winston Churchill

'May you be in heaven a full half-hour before the Devil knows you're dead.'

– Michael Shelby

'Your lethal hand is always on our shoulders.'

– Ada Thorne

'Even on holiday, even on top of a rocky mountain, he'll be the same way he's been since Polly died. No more Polly, no more whisky, no more Tommy.'

– Freddie Thorne

'[Character], you're dead!' – Alfie Solomons
'No. I've been living in London. Same thing.'

– Grace Burgess

'I really must come up to Birmingham someday and spend an evening with your family. They sound interesting.'

– Irene O'Donnell

'Don't fuck with the Peaky Blinders.'

– Arthur Shelby

'Life is so much easier to deal with when you are dead.'

– Danny Whizz-Bang

'The one minute. The soldier's minute. In a battle, that's all you get. One minute of everything at once. And anything before is nothing. Everything after, nothing. Nothing in comparison to that one minute.'

– Father John Hughes

'They killed him. My son. They shot him and they put him on a fucking cross and he's fucking dead.'

– Polly Gray

'I'm an old man and my heart's a battered vessel, but within, there still beats a fluttering pulse of a dream.'

– Chester Campbell

'We're a close family, always within punching distance.'

– Arthur Shelby

'In all the world, violent men are the easiest to deal with.'

– Grace Burgess

'There's God, and there are the Peaky Blinders.'

– Tommy Shelby

ANSWERS

SERIES ONE: EPISODE ONE

1. a
2. b
3. c
4. a – extra point for knowing he's turning eleven on the coming Sunday
5. b
6. a
7. c
8. b
9. c
10. a
11. a
12. b
13. c
14. c – Specifically, Irish Protestants, according to Arthur
15. a
16. a
17. b – Discretionary points for knowing: 25 Lewis machine guns, 10,000 rounds of ammunition, 50 semi-automatic rifles and 200 pistols with shells, supposed to be on their way to Libya.

18. a
19. b
20. c
21. a
22. c
23. a
24. c
25. a

SERIES ONE: EPISODE TWO

1. a – Johnny gets a go in the car after losing a game of two-up
2. Tommy, John and Arthur
3. a
4. b
5. c
6. c – He says she looked foot-sore
7. a
8. b
9. b
10. c
11. a
12. c
13. a
14. b
15. c
16. a
17. a
18. b
19. b
20. a

CILLIAN MURPHY

1. a
2. a
3. b – Originally a village in its own right but incorporated into the city of Cork in 2019
4. c – Another incorporated village
5. b
6. a

7. a. By the way, we're aware that The Sultans have had many different versions of their name over the years – this is the one we like the best, though
8. b
9. c
10. c
11. a
12. a. Extra discretionary point for knowing the writer is Enda Walsh, who later collaborated with David Bowie, no less
13. c
14. c
15. b
16. c
17. c – But hey, wouldn't you love to see b)?
18. c
19. b
20. a
21. c
22. b – Again, let's make c) happen though, please
23. a
24. c
25. b

SERIES ONE: EPISODE THREE

1. b – aka The IRA
2. b
3. b
4. a
5. c
6. c
7. c

8. c
9. b
10. c
11. a
12. a
13. a
14. b
15. b
16. a
17. a
18. a
19. a
20. a

SERIES ONE: EPISODE FOUR

1. a
2. a
3. b
4. c – That is, she's only ever made money horizontally – lying on her back as a prostitute
5. b
6. a – In France, the retreating Allies would booby trap their previous frontline position in the same way
7. b – Though, of course, both the other options aren't bad advice either
8. b
9. b – So it's actually family business
10. c
11. a
12. a
13. a

14. a
15. b
16. c
17. a
18. b
19. c
20. b

SERIES ONE: EPISODE FIVE

1. b
2. c
3. b
4. a
5. b
6. a, b and c – A trick question – Arthur Snr is dad to all those lads
7. b
8. c
9. c
10. c
11. a
12. c
13. c
14. a
15. a
16. b
17. a
18. b
19. a
20. c

SERIES ONE: EPISODE SIX

1. b
2. c
3. b
4. a
5. a
6. b
7. a
8. b
9. b

10. a
11. a
12. c
13. b
14. a
15. a
16. b – Also accept 'The soldier's minute' from his famous lines here
17. c
18. a
19. a – And the men disperse. They all look sick of fighting. Tommy has also taken a bullet, but it's removed in the pub by his men
20. b

SERIES ONE: SOUNDTRACK

1. a
2. b
3. c
4. c
5. b
6. b
7. a
8. c
9. a
10. b

SERIES TWO: EPISODE ONE

1. b
2. a – In other words, flu/illness; both acceptable answers
3. c
4. a
5. a
6. b – Heroic work
7. c
8. b
9. a – So Campbell survived the gunshot at the end of the last series
10. a

11. c
12. a
13. b
14. b – Poor Polly
15. b – To the Blinders' confusion
16. a – That is to say, per the Bible, those who are being exploited will see their fortunes increase
17. b
18. b
19. b
20. c – We're right back into the intrigue with everyone's plans and schemes overlapping, folks. Strap in!

SERIES TWO: EPISODE TWO

1. a
2. a
3. b
4. c
5. c
6. c
7. a
8. a
9. a
10. c
11. a
12. b
13. b
14. a
15. c
16. b – Pub quiz fact: 'soupçon' is French for 'suspicion'
17. c – There's definitely a spin-off series to be had about Anna's antics sometime! All we need is 10 per cent for the idea. Gross, not net
18. b – Cocaine
19. c
20. b

SAM NEILL

1. c
2. c
3. a
4. a – Sir Nigel John Dermot Neill, Knight Companion of the New Zealand Order of Merit (KNZM), Officer of the Most Excellent Order of the British Empire (OBE)
5. b
6. a
7. c
8. a
9. b
10. c
11. c
12. b
13. a
14. a
15. b
16. b
17. a – He was reunited with his son in 1994 (who had been put up for adoption) and also adopted Maiko Watanabe, daughter of his second wife, Noriko
18. c
19. a – As told to Kelly Clarkson on her eponymous show in April 2024
20. a

SERIES TWO: EPISODE THREE

1. a
2. b
3. c
4. c
5. b
6. b
7. c
8. b
9. a – Yep, all very *Fight Club*, innit?
10. a
11. a
12. b
13. b
14. a
15. a
16. a
17. c
18. a
19. a
20. b

SERIES TWO: EPISODE FOUR

1. c
2. a
3. b
4. a
5. b
6. b – Somewhat facetiously
7. c
8. c
9. a
10. b
11. c
12. a
13. b
14. a
15. a
16. a
17. c
18. b
19. b – In a very revealing conversation we also find out that Alfie and Darby have been arguing and making up again since they were kids so the bonds are a lot stronger than Tommy realises
20. b – The barman sets him straight that Michael is a Shelby, but it's not enough. Cue the pub duly going up in flames...

SPEAKY BLINDERS

Word – Definition

Peaky – A flat cap with a peak

Blinder – Stylish, dapper, generally great ('blinding')/Member of a gang that takes eyes

Snow – Cocaine

Up the duff – Pregnant

The clap – Sexually transmitted disease, generally syphilis (though, yes, 'Up the duff' is also technically sexually transmitted, but we won't call being with child a disease!)

Bookie – Bookmaker

Chalkers and rafflers – Those who write odds on the bookie's chalk boards, and those who write the betting slips

The cut – Canal

Flanders Blues – A kind of World War I PTSD, known after World War II as 'shell shock'
Parley – A scheduled discussion, particularly between rivals

SERIES TWO: EPISODE FIVE

1. a
2. b
3. c
4. c
5. b – He says they will eat the worm eggs
6. b
7. a
8. b
9. a
10. b
11. a – And given the revelation that pre-war, he wanted to work with horses, perhaps it's to soothe himself too
12. b
13. a
14. b – This is a huge and enticing story that came to light after Chaplin's oldest surviving son, Michael, seemed to say a letter signed by Jack Hill, a Romani, existed. Furthermore, Charlie Chaplin kept it locked in a bedside table; it was only discovered after the death of his wife Oona O'Neill in 1991, then kept in a vault in Montreux; indeed, Charlie's birth certificate has never been revealed (or found). Oh, for a posthumous *Who Do You Think You Are?* episode...
15. c
16. a
17. c – As she says, she intends to win Tommy despite his revelations that he's seen Grace
18. a

19. a
20. b – Rather than being caught in a trap near Russell's residence, Tommy now has a smidgin of protection from being killed in his turn

SERIES TWO: EPISODE SIX

1. c
2. a
3. b – 'For the cause' apparently
4. a – Suspicious? Nahhhh!
5. b
6. a
7. a – A massive bluff based on James' presence and Tommy's war record. He and Alfie agree on 35 per cent in the end, and all walk away, unharmed. High stakes, so never play poker with Tommy Shelby, folks. It won't end well for you
8. c
9. b
10. a
11. c
12. a
13. a
14. a
15. b
16. b
17. c
18. b
19. c – What a revenge scene. Go, Polly! And, let's not forget – what an actress!
20. As Tommy is kneeling before the grave, one of the three kidnappers shoots the other two. That man then tells Tommy that Winston Churchill wants to speak to the Peaky Blinder head himself.

Tommy walks away and doesn't look back. Folks, this is simply wonderful drama by anyone's standards

SERIES TWO: SOUNDTRACK

1. a
2. b
3. c
4. a
5. a
6. b
7. c
8. b
9. a
10. b

SERIES THREE: EPISODE ONE

1. a
2. b – Usually a phrase said by Tommy or a Blinder when someone is about to die; specifically the Blinders that were part of the Small Heath Rifles; specifically those who were once stuck in a foxhole waiting for the enemy
3. b
4. b
5. c
6. a
7. c
8. a
9. b
10. c
11. b
12. c – Though it's a fairly good bet that all three are true by this stage
13. b
14. c
15. c
16. a
17. a

18. c
19. a
20. a

SERIES THREE: EPISODE TWO

1. a
2. a
3. b
4. c
5. c
6. b
7. c
8. b
9. c
10. a
11. b
12. c
13. a, b and c. For such an incredible show these moments really are a bit silly
14. b
15. a
16. c
17. a
18. b
19. c
20. b

HELEN McCRORY

1. a
2. b
3. c
4. b
5. *Deep breath* Oscar Fingal O'Fflahertie Wills Wilde. That third name's spelling is inconsistent on many different sources from his actual life, so don't be too harsh when awarding points (unless you're a fiendish person, in which case an evil laugh is acceptable)
6. b – Bonus fact, the author of this book wrote an essay for his GCSE English in which he referred more than once to the non-existent character 'Thelonius' in *A Midsummer Night's Dream*. He was thinking of Thelonious Monk, the jazz pianist and singer, for some reason. So, y'know. Don't fret too much about exams, kids

7. a
8. a – She received a nomination for a Laurence Olivier Award for this one, so if anyone ventures that answer, give them a point at your discretion
9. c
10. b – Married, of course, to then-Prime Minister, Tony Blair
11. a
12. *Harry Potter and the Half-Blood Prince*; *Harry Potter and the Deathly Hallows Part I*; *Harry Potter and the Deathly Hallows Part II*. Released in 2009, 2010 and 2011 respectively
13. a
14. c
15. c
16. a – Wonderful work!
17. b
18. c
19. c
20. *Charlotte*. It was about the life of Charlotte Salomon

SERIES THREE: EPISODE THREE

1. a
2. b
3. b
4. a
5. c
6. b
7. a
8. c
9. c
10. a
11. b
12. a
13. a
14. b
15. a
16. b
17. a
18. a
19. c
20. c

SERIES THREE: EPISODE FOUR

1. a
2. c
3. a
4. b
5. c
6. a
7. b
8. b
9. a
10. a
11. b
12. b – Not that she's too upset about the prospect
13. a – Or, rather, Georgian in this case
14. c – In a cellar which they've turned into a strong room
15. b – He's there to keep his ears open for the Peaky Blinders
16. c
17. b
18. a
19. c
20. c

PAUL ANDERSON

1. b – No apologies for the fiendish choice between A and B here, it's Peaky f-in Blinders! (Oh, OK, we are sorry and love you very much)
2. a
3. c – Paul has mentioned this in various interviews
4. c
5. a
6. b
7. b
8. c
9. a
10. b
11. His character was called Anderson
12. a
13. b
14. b

15. c
16. a – We'd love to see c, though
17. b
18. c
19. a
20. b

SERIES THREE: EPISODE FIVE

1. c
2. c
3. Tommy was starting to hallucinate Mary reading the Book of Leviticus from the Bible, naked, standing next to his bed
4. a
5. b
6. c
7. a
8. b – The sense of repressed violence is palpable
9. b
10. To show the Romanovs that they do not have any tattoos linking them to anti-royal organisations, as is customary in Russia (according to Tommy, anyway)
11. b
12. c
13. a
14. a
15. b
16. a
17. c – And it doesn't even have chocolate buttons in the middle either. Weirdoes!
18. b
19. c – Specifically, they'd surreptitiously tunnel towards German

lines in the Great War (World War I) and be incredibly quiet about it; once the tunnels were in place, explosives could be put there which would then be set off, obliterating the enemy

20. a

SERIES THREE: EPISODE SIX

1. a
2. b
3. b
4. c
5. a
6. b
7. a
8. b
9. b
10. a
11. b
12. a
13. b
14. c
15. c
16. a
17. a
18. c – Michael proves himself, literally, a Blinder, before finishing Hughes off by cutting his throat
19. a – That is to say, from the lower classes; from gypsy and Irish stock; from humble beginnings etc.
20. c – The Odd Fellows, the establishment and so on want to make the Peaky Blinders pay. Tommy, though, says he has already made a deal of some sort… sounds like a new series to me

SERIES THREE: SOUNDTRACK

1. a – And what a magnificent piece of work it truly is
2. b – And what a magnificent piece of work it truly is
3. b – And what a... etc.
4. c – A point for knowing that Zowie was one of his kids, and that Derek Dick is the real name of Fish (once of Marillion fame)
5. c
6. c
7. b
8. c
9. a
10. b ('Don't Sit Down Cause I've Moved Your Chair', from their 2011 LP, *Suck It And See*)

SERIES FOUR: EPISODE ONE

1. b
2. c
3. a
4. a
5. a
6. b
7. b
8. c
9. a
10. b
11. a
12. b
13. c
14. a – Bad, bad news: it's a Mafia promise that they are on a hitlist and will be killed by The Black Hand
15. b
16. a
17. a – Note that at this point Tommy has taken off his glasses of respectability, too
18. b
19. a
20. b

SERIES FOUR: EPISODE TWO

1. a
2. b – That is to say, back to her Romani travelling family and life
3. b
4. a
5. b
6. b
7. a
8. c
9. c
10. c
11. a
12. b
13. a
14. c
15. a – To train the horse
16. c
17. a
18. a
19. b
20. a

ANNABELLE WALLIS

1. b
2. b – 25 September 1984
3. a – Oxford!
4. c
5. c – Lee was unavailable due to other commitments and, anecdotally, McKellen turned it down as Harris had once called him 'dreadful' as an actor!
6. c
7. b
8. b
9. a
10. b
11. b
12. b – Perfect casting!
13. c
14. c – A reboot of the famous franchise
15. c

16. a – A deliciously silly movie in which she plays Emily May/ Madison Mitchell
17. b
18. c – In Italian, it's *Svaniti Nella Notte*, if anyone's showing off
19. a – Save the Children and No Kid Hungry were also involved in #SaveWith Stories
20. c

SERIES FOUR: EPISODE THREE

1. c
2. c
3. a
4. b
5. Six years previously, Luca had travelled to his cousin's wedding in Birmingham, to be best man. The photographers were Reid and Dunn, on Broadgate. As the photographer kept the negatives, it was possible for Polly to get hold of copies of the pics and to enlarge the one of Luca
6. a
7. a
8. a
9. b
10. a
11. b
12. a
13. a
14. a
15. b
16. c
17. b
18. a
19. a
20. c

SERIES FOUR: EPISODE FOUR

1. b
2. a
3. c
4. a

5. c
6. a
7. b – Extra point if anyone correctly says it was in 1833
8. c
9. c
10. b – In other words, it's worth as much as he'd like to fill in
11. c
12. b
13. b – Hence why she needs to change from whisky to stout
14. c
15. c
16. c
17. c
18. b
19. b
20. c

JOE COLE

1. c
2. b
3. b
4. c – Sometimes a mounted archer, or even a centaur (half man, half horse). You could say Joe Cole was a centaur forward, but that'd be a rubbish joke so please don't!
5. c
6. a
7. a
8. b
9. c
10. b – Harry Palmer

SERIES FOUR: EPISODE FIVE

1. a
2. a
3. c
4. a
5. b
6. b
7. b
8. c
9. c
10. b
11. a – He says he has a blind cousin, and thus donates money to a charity that gives guide dogs to blind Jews
12. c
13. b
14. a
15. c
16. b
17. c
18. a
19. b
20. c

SERIES FOUR: EPISODE SIX

1. b
2. b
3. c
4. b
5. a
6. c
7. a – Thus becoming, finally, an actual Blinder
8. c
9. b
10. a
11. a
12. b
13. c – Al Capone, of course. Come on, what a brilliant twist!
14. a
15. b – Whoo! Another incredible Tommy plan works out
16. b
17. a
18. c
19. a
20. c – What a series ending!

SERIES FOUR: SOUNDTRACK

1. a
2. b
3. c
4. a
5. c
6. b
7. c
8. b
9. b
10. a

SERIES FIVE: EPISODE ONE

1. a
2. c
3. b
4. a – That is, Romani
5. a
6. a
7. b
8. b
9. c
10. c
11. a
12. b
13. a
14. b
15. c
16. A High Court judge, Scotland Yard, and the House of Lords
17. b
18. c – Also, carry their own can and pay their own bills. Discretionary extra points if you're feeling warmth for your comrades
19. c
20. a

SERIES FIVE: EPISODE TWO

1. b
2. c
3. a
4. b
5. c – The Ulster Volunteer Force; a loyalist (to the Crown) paramilitary group at odds with the IRA
6. b
7. a
8. a – According to the Naval Marriages Act, 1908 and in certain circumstances. It was partly repealed in 1949
9. a
10. b
11. c
12. A black cat. That signifies that there is a traitor at hand. It could also mean that he's hurting or betraying himself
13. c
14. b
15. a
16. b
17. b – Extremely brutally, too
18. a
19. a
20. b

SOPHIE RUNDLE

1. c
2. a
3. a – Commonly known as RADA, so a point for that too
4. c
5. b

6. c
7. a
8. b
9. c
10. b
11. c
12. b – Sufferers believe they are already dead or perhaps rotting away right there. Another version is that people feel immortal
13. a
14. a
15. b
16. a – The book's called *Good Vibrations: The True Story of Ann Summers*
17. c
18. c – In Sky's 2019 *Urban Myths*
19. a
20. a

SERIES FIVE: EPISODE THREE

1. a
2. a
3. b
4. b
5. c
6. b
7. c
8. b
9. c
10. c
11. a
12. c
13. b
14. a – In fact, she wants to have the baby in New York
15. a
16. b
17. c
18. c
19. a
20. c

SERIES FIVE: EPISODE FOUR

1. a
2. c
3. c
4. b
5. c
6. b
7. b
8. c
9. a – The fee the Blinders will get is £250,000; the amount Michael lost in the Wall Street Crash is £500,000
10. a
11. b
12. b
13. c – His father's boat
14. a
15. c
16. b
17. a
18. b
19. c
20. c

NED DENNEHY

1. b – 8 December 1965
2. b
3. a
4. c
5. c
6. a
7. b – Also accept 'Irish Pat'
8. c
9. b
10. a

SERIES FIVE: EPISODE FIVE

1. b
2. a
3. b
4. b
5. a
6. c
7. a
8. c
9. b
10. b
11. a
12. a
13. c
14. a
15. b
16. c
17. b
18. b
19. a
20. a

SERIES FIVE: EPISODE SIX

1. a
2. b
3. c
4. b
5. a
6. b
7. a
8. b
9. c
10. c
11. a
12. b
13. a
14. a
15. a – This is a river that flows through Hades, in Greek myth, and the one that the souls of the dead drink from to forget their previous/earthly lives. In this case it also highlights that Alfie, being dead in the eyes of the world, is able to be forgotten and have an easier final months of his life (he revealed he had advanced cancer the last time we saw him, where Tommy shot him supposedly dead)
16. a
17. b
18. a
19. a – Barney is to count to 10, then shoot
20. b

SERIES FIVE: SOUNDTRACK

1. b
2. b
3. a
4. a, b and certainly c
5. c
6. a
7. c – She was a background singer for various acts including Ike and Tina, Joe Cocker, Freddie King, Humble Pie and Leon Russell – and released one album in her own right in 1973. Lennear dated Bowie for a while, and previously had been seeing Mick Jagger. The Stones' 'Brown Sugar' is also apparently inspired by her. Some legacy! Oh, and if anyone knows any of this, give 'em a buncha points, unless they're all cocky about it, in which case take some away. You're the boss!
8. b
9. a
10. c

SERIES SIX: EPISODE ONE

1. b
2. a
3. b – Soldiers from three brigades of the Irish Republican Army, from Dublin
4. a
5. a
6. b
7. b
8. c – And that it's a Black Day for Miquelon (because many of the islanders made their money bootlegging under Prohibition and now will have no source of income)

9. b
10. c
11. a
12. a – Technically, French territory
13. c
14. a
15. b
16. c
17. c
18. a
19. a
20. a – In Romani, something like 'The Devil will take the little girl', though it's not a direct translation. It's firmly *not* good news, though

SERIES SIX: EPISODE TWO

1. a
2. b
3. c
4. b
5. a
6. b – What a great speech he's given to rouse everyone, don't you think?
7. a – Also known as Captain Swing, so an extra point available here
8. c
9. b
10. a – In fact, proof that his beloved Fascism will come to pass
11. b
12. c
13. b
14. b
15. b – Another great Tommy quote is that the way of the people of the UK is compromise
16. a
17. b
18. a
19. b
20. a

NATASHA O'KEEFFE

1. b
2. a
3. c
4. c
5. c
6. c
7. b
8. a
9. a – It's quite an extraordinary coincidence, or perhaps better to say the world of Holmes has a lot in common with the atmosphere and time in which *Peaky Blinders* is set
10. b
11. c
12. c
13. b
14. b
15. a
16. b – Based on the series of novels about titular hero Cormoran Strike
17. b
18. a
19. c
20. b

SERIES SIX: EPISODE THREE

1. a – That is, tuberculosis
2. b
3. a
4. c
5. a

6. c
7. c
8. b
9. b
10. a
11. b
12. c
13. b
14. c
15. c
16. a
17. a, b and c. Perfect for the show!
18. a
19. a
20. b

SERIES SIX: EPISODE FOUR

1. a
2. a
3. c
4. b
5. b
6. a
7. a
8. b
9. b – And has been rooting for him to win ever since
10. a
11. c
12. a – She actually says 'The Chancellor', meaning Hitler. She's properly, properly horrendous, this one
13. c
14. a
15. b
16. c – That is, opium/heroin
17. b
18. a
19. a
20. b

BENJAMIN ZEPHANIAH

1. a
2. b – Handsworth, to be exact
3. a
4. a
5. b
6. a
7. b
8. b
9. c
10. b
11. c – Benjamin was the only Top 10 poet to still be alive at the time
12. b – The 2004 New Year Honours List. Benjamin told *The Guardian* that he was 'profoundly anti-empire'. No doubt he would have rejected any of the honours listed in the question for the same reasons. The full interview is very much worth a look if you can find it
13. c – He'd been vegan since around age 13 (and this also ties in with some Rastafarian beliefs)
14. a
15. c
16. a – As presented by Koestler Arts
17. a
18. c
19. a – He later described himself as a 'rasta folkie', though
20. b – His second wife was a Chinese lady called Qian Zheng

SERIES SIX: EPISODE FIVE

1. b
2. a
3. c
4. b
5. b
6. a
7. b
8. a
9. b
10. b
11. a
12. b
13. c
14. a
15. c – Under duress, but becoming a Peaky Blinder as a result
16. a
17. a
18. c
19. b
20. c – Polly herself, or at least her spirit. She transcends life and death in many ways

SERIES SIX: EPISODE SIX

1. c
2. a
3. b
4. a
5. b
6. c
7. b
8. a
9. b
10. b
11. a
12. c
13. b
14. a
15. c
16. c

17. c
18. c
19. c
20. b – He can't bring himself to kill Billy, to whom he has become close
21. b
22. a – Recalling the terrible Third Battle of Ypres, or as Arthur refers to it: Passchendaele
23. b
24. a – Tommy's lethal hand is always on their shoulders, he elaborates
25. b – The Peaky Blinders' boss giving another lesson in blinding his enemies
26. c
27. a
28. b
29. c
30. Tommy puts the gun to his head and says, 'In the bleak midwinter' as if he's about to shoot himself. Then he has a vision of Ruby, who runs to him and tells him he's not dead – in fact, he's not even sick. She tells him to light the fire which has gone out, and that in doing so, he will see that he must in fact live. Tommy picks up a newspaper to do just that – and sees a photo of the Mosleys' wedding. In the photo are both his doctor and the doctor who gave him a second opinion. Tommy deduces that in fact they were both lying to him and he is *not* dying. The only person who could ever kill Tommy was Tommy himself; he goes to put a bullet in the head of Doctor Holford. But Tommy does not do so, but instead rides away on a white horse as his carriage goes up in flames. It is a metaphorical death and, as Alfie also says, there are benefits to everyone thinking that you are dead when you're still very much alive. So, folks, give as many points as you wish for the answer, and get ready for one hell of a movie!

SERIES SIX: SOUNDTRACK

1. a
2. c – Particularly if you do, in fact, give it the full nine yards and treat your compadres to your own version
3. c – Written specially for the series, no less
4. b
5. c
6. b
7. b
8. c
9. b
10. c

BY ORDER OF... WHO? QUOTES QUIZ

'Men always tell their troubles to a barmaid.' – Grace Burgess

'When you're dead already, you're free.' – Polly Gray

'I heard you dress well, Mr Shelby. But now I see, not so well as me.' – Luca Changretta

'There is good in my heart, but these hands belong to the Devil.' – Arthur Shelby

'Men like us, Mr Shelby, will always be alone. And what love we get, we will have to pay for.' – Chester Campbell

'May you be in heaven a full half-hour before the Devil knows you're dead.' – Grace Burgess [Note: this is a wonderful old Irish saying used generally as a toast]

'Your lethal hand is always on our shoulders.' – Michael Shelby

'Even on holiday, even on top of a rocky mountain, he'll be the same way he's been since Polly died. No more Polly, no more whisky, no more Tommy.' – Lizzie Shelby

'Danny, you're dead!' – Freddie Thorne [Note: give an extra point for knowing the name in the full quote]

'No. I've been living in London. Same thing.' – Danny Whizz-Bang

'I really must come up to Birmingham someday and spend an evening with your family. They sound interesting.' – Winston Churchill

'Don't fuck with the Peaky Blinders.' – Polly Gray

'Life is so much easier to deal with when you are dead.' – Alfie Solomons

'The one minute. The soldier's minute. In a battle, that's all you get. One minute of everything at once. And anything before is nothing. Everything after, nothing. Nothing in comparison to that one minute.' – Tommy Shelby

'They killed him. My son. They shot him and they put him on a fucking cross and he's fucking dead.' – Aberama Gold

'I'm an old man and my heart's a battered vessel, but within, there still beats a fluttering pulse of a dream.' – Arthur Shelby

'We're a close family, always within punching distance.' – Ada Thorne

'In all the world, violent men are the easiest to deal with.' – Irene O'Donnell

'There's God, and there are the Peaky Blinders.' – Father John Hughes

ACKNOWLEDGEMENTS

Thanks to Suzy and the boys; colleagues and friends; Ciara, Saira and Bonnier Books.

Generative AI was NOT used in any part of the creation of this book. Data scraping for model training is theft and should we find out this book's been used for that purpose, we're going to send in some madheads in peaked caps with razor blades sewn into them. Figuratively speaking, of course.

Use your local library.

No human is illegal.